Time Management

Reducing Stress Through Effective Time Management

(Simple Strategies to Increase Productivity and Make Your Time Your Own)

Anton McCloud

Published By **Darby Connor**

Anton McCloud

Time Management: Reducing Stress Through Effective Time Management (Simple Strategies to Increase Productivity and Make Your Time Your Own)

ISBN 978-1-9990334-4-6

No part of this guidebook shall be reproduced in any form without permission in writing from the publisher except in the case of brief quotations embodied in critical articles or reviews.

Legal & Disclaimer

The information contained in this book is not designed to replace or take the place of any form of medicine or professional medical advice. The information in this book has been provided for educational & entertainment purposes only.

The information contained in this book has been compiled from sources deemed reliable, and it is accurate to the best of the Author's knowledge; however, the Author cannot guarantee its accuracy and validity and cannot be held liable for any errors or omissions. Changes are periodically made to this book. You must consult your doctor or get professional medical advice before using any of the suggested remedies, techniques, or information in this book.

Upon using the information contained in this book, you agree to hold harmless the Author from and against any damages, costs, and expenses, including any legal fees potentially resulting from the application of any of the information provided by this guide. This disclaimer applies to any damages or injury caused by the use and application, whether directly or indirectly, of any advice or information presented, whether for breach of contract, tort, negligence, personal injury, criminal intent, or under any other cause of action.

You agree to accept all risks of using the information presented inside this book. You need to consult a professional medical practitioner in order to ensure you are both able and healthy enough to participate in this program.

Table Of Contents

Chapter 1: Setting Clear Goals and Priorities

The 2d financial disaster of "Time Management for Dummies" is dedicated to the essential building blocks of powerful time management: setting smooth dreams and putting in area priorities. In this crucial chapter, the writer delves into the paintings of defining your dreams, making them measurable and actionable, and information the importance of prioritizing obligations to benefit your goals effectively.

Understanding the Power of Clear Goals:

Understanding the power of clean dreams is paramount in powerful time management. Clear dreams offer a feel of route, reason, and motivation. They feature a roadmap for our actions, assisting us prioritize responsibilities, allocate property, and make knowledgeable choices. Clear goals allow people to set precise, measurable, practicable, applicable, and time-positive (SMART) goals, improving their functionality to diploma progress and stay on course. With a strong maintain close of the significance of clean desires, human beings can navigate their time control adventure with goal, making sure that every step taken aligns with their broader imaginative and prescient and aspirations.

The SMART Criteria:

The SMART requirements are a treasured framework for putting desires which is probably Specific, Measurable, Achievable, Relevant, and Time-certain. Specific desires are smooth and nicely-described, leaving no room for ambiguity. Measurable dreams have quantifiable symptoms to tune development. Achievable dreams are realistic and potential given the available assets and constraints. Relevant goals are aligned with one's broader dreams and priorities. Time-certain goals have a fixed cut-off date, growing a experience of urgency and willpower. By adhering to the SMART requirements, individuals can craft dreams which might be more actionable and probably to purpose a achievement outcomes.

Creating a Goal Hierarchy:

Creating a purpose hierarchy is a strategic manner that entails breaking down overarching goals into smaller, extra potential sub-goals. It allows human beings to visualize the steps required to attain their remaining dreams and offers a smooth roadmap for improvement. This hierarchical structure permits a feel of awareness and course, supporting human beings prioritize their efforts, allocate resources appropriately, and degree their development successfully. By building a reason hierarchy, human beings can navigate their adventure with clarity, making sure that each sub-purpose they triumph over leads them in the direction of the belief of their large aspirations.

The Eisenhower Matrix:

The Eisenhower Matrix, a time manage tool named after President Dwight D. Eisenhower, is a smooth yet powerful manner to prioritize duties based totally totally on their urgency and importance. This matrix categorizes duties into four quadrants: critical and urgent, vital however not pressing, pressing however now not essential, and neither urgent nor important. By classifying responsibilities on this manner, individuals should make informed alternatives about what to awareness on first, what to delegate, what to time desk for later, and what to put off. The Eisenhower Matrix is a treasured tool for boosting productivity and making sure that critical obligations receive the attention they deserve, while heaps much less vital ones are because it must be controlled, in the end important to better time manipulate and choice-making.

The 80/20 Rule:

The eighty/20 rule, additionally referred to as the Pareto Principle, is a profound idea that shows 80% of results result from 20% of efforts or motives. Named after Italian economist Vilfredo Pareto, this precept may be implemented to severa elements of life, consisting of time manipulate. It encourages people to discover and popularity on the most extensive responsibilities or elements that yield the most tremendous consequences. By the usage of the 80/20 rule to their time control practices, people can pinpoint the most impactful sports and prioritize them, thinking about a greater efficient and effective use in their time, ultimately main to extended productivity and better outcomes.

Time Blocking and Goal Alignment:

Time blocking is a time management method that includes scheduling specific blocks of time for diverse obligations and sports sports at a few level within the day. When mixed with intention alignment, it will become a powerful method for conducting one's goals. By aligning time blocks with the proper desires or responsibilities related to the ones desires, people can make sure that they're dedicating targeted, uninterrupted intervals to the maximum essential sports activities activities that pressure them inside the direction in their favored consequences. This synergy among time blocking off and purpose alignment lets in for a primarily based and intentional approach to time manage, making sure that each day is devoted to significant steps that align with one's overarching goals.

Overcoming Goal-Setting Challenges:

Overcoming aim-setting annoying conditions is a crucial factor of effective time control and personal development. Setting dreams can be difficult due to elements like uncertainty, fear of failure, or putting unrealistic expectancies. To deal with the ones traumatic situations, human beings can damage down their goals into smaller, extra potential steps, thinking about a enjoy of achievement alongside the way. Additionally, staying adaptable and open to revisions within the face of converting conditions is important. Seeking manual, obligation, and self-mirrored image are crucial techniques in overcoming goal-putting barriers, in the end making sure that people can set and reap their goals with self perception and fulfillment.

Tools and Resources for Goal Setting:

Concludes with a discussion of severa gadget and resources that could assist in setting and monitoring desires. It highlights the importance of era and time manipulate apps, reason-setting journals, and exquisite assets that might streamline the manner of putting and reaching dreams. The author presents pointers for specific tools and explains the way to combine them into some time management technique.

Visualizing Your Goals:

Emphasizes the power of visualization in cause setting. Visualizing your desires approach growing a highbrow image of your selected outcomes. This technique permits in making your desires extra tangible and motivating. By visualizing your dreams, you could beef up your self-discipline to accomplishing them. The creator gives carrying sports activities and examples to assist readers exercise this vital capability.

Goal Setting for Different Areas of Life:

The significance of putting desires in severa areas of existence, at the facet of career, personal development, health, and relationships. It discusses the concept that a nicely-rounded approach to intention putting effects in a balanced and high-quality existence. Readers are advocated to define their dreams in those various factors of existence, and realistic suggestions are provided for retaining equilibrium among them.

Chapter 2: Creating a Time Management Plan

In Chapter three of "Time Management for Dummies," the focal point shifts to the practical software program software of time manage standards. Setting clean goals and priorities, as stated within the preceding monetary damage, lays the foundation for effective time control. In this bankruptcy, readers learn how to transform the ones dreams proper right right into a established and actionable time control plan.

The Importance of Planning:

Emphasizing the significance of making plans inside the realm of time management. Planning is like the blueprint in your day, week, or month, and it serves due to the fact the framework upon which you may assemble your fulfillment. Without a properly-notion-out plan, you could discover yourself reacting to conditions in choice to proactively handling a while. The creator explains that a well-crafted time management plan is the crucial thing to maximizing productiveness and carrying out your desires.

Components of a Time Management Plan:

A time manipulate plan generally includes numerous key additives. These additives encompass:

Prioritization: The writer reiterates the significance of setting easy priorities. Understanding which obligations are maximum vital and time-touchy is the first step in powerful planning. By the use of techniques just like the Eisenhower Matrix or the 80/20 rule, readers can decide what merits their on the spot interest.

Goal Alignment: Goal alignment is the way of making sure that character obligations, sports, and priorities are in concord with one's overarching dreams and dreams. It's about making deliberate alternatives to reputation on sports that immediately make a contribution to the fulfillment of those goals. By aligning every day movements with extended-term aspirations, humans can maximize their time control efforts and art work within the direction of identifying their favored results successfully. Goal alignment serves as a compass, guiding people of their each day desire-making and ensuring that their time and strength are invested in pastimes that rely maximum to them.

Time Blocking: Time blocking off is a high-quality time management approach that consists of breaking one's day into unique blocks of time, each committed to a selected project or hobby. This based totally definitely technique allows humans to allocate targeted, uninterrupted durations for their most vital obligations. By segmenting the day and assigning time blocks to obligations, time blocking complements productivity and allows people make the most in their to be had hours. It affords a smooth roadmap for coping with every day commitments and fosters a sense of success as every time block is successfully finished. Time blockading is a flexible tool for optimizing time manipulate, making it an important technique for every personal and expert effectiveness.

Scheduling: Scheduling is a essential issue of powerful time control. It includes allocating unique time slots for diverse duties and sports, ensuring that one's day is primarily based and organized. Scheduling lets in humans manipulate their time efficaciously, prevent overcommitment, and ensure that important priorities are addressed. It lets in the balancing of labor, personal life, and self-care with the aid of designating committed time for every. Through scheduling, humans advantage a clearer sense of manipulate over their time and may make the maximum in their day at the equal time as lowering stress and chaos.

To-Do Lists: To-do lists are beneficial gear in time manage. They offer a hooked up way to set up responsibilities and prioritize them primarily based totally on urgency and significance. These lists function a seen manual, making sure that people can song their daily, weekly, or prolonged-term goals and live on top of last dates. By developing and often updating to-do lists, people can boom their productiveness, lessen the risk of forgetting important duties, and enjoy a revel in of achievement as they check off finished objects. To-do lists are easy however powerful aids that help people take manage of their time and manipulate their commitments extra efficaciously.

Creating a Weekly Time Management Plan:

Creating a weekly time management plan is an crucial tool for optimizing productiveness and staying organized. It includes placing particular goals for the week, breaking them down into each day obligations, and allocating time blocks for each interest. A well-set up weekly plan helps human beings see the larger picture, letting them prioritize obligations and control their time successfully. It offers a roadmap for the week beforehand, reducing pressure and making sure that essential duties get hold of the eye they deserve. By proactively growing a weekly time manage plan, human beings can align their moves with their goals and make the maximum in their time.

Avoiding Overloading Your Schedule:

Avoiding overloading it sluggish desk is a crucial detail of effective time manage. Overloading can result in strain, burnout, and reduced productiveness. It's crucial to understand one's obstacles and set sensible expectancies for what can be performed in a given time frame. By prioritizing obligations and learning to say no, on the identical time as critical, individuals can save you the crush that consists of an overloaded agenda. This method permits for a greater match work-existence balance, expanded attention on vital obligations, and in the end, higher time manipulate effects.

Dealing with Unexpected Events:

Dealing with unexpected events is a essential element of powerful time management. Life is inherently unpredictable, and surprising times can disrupt even the maximum well-deliberate schedules. To navigate these demanding conditions, people have to stay adaptable and creative. This consists of having contingency plans, placing aside buffer time in schedules, and being mentally prepared to shift priorities as favored. By drawing near unexpected events with a bendy mind-set and a proactive approach, people can mitigate disruptions, lessen strain, and hold a experience of manage over their time and productivity.

Time Management Tools and Resources:

Time control device and property are treasured property for enhancing one's capability to control time effectively. These gear embody a enormous sort of property, from virtual apps and software software software program to physical planners and strategies. They useful resource human beings in organizing, prioritizing, and scheduling responsibilities and activities, facilitating higher time allocation. Time control equipment and assets offer shape, assist in tracking progress, and offer reminders, allowing people to stay on pinnacle of their commitments and goals. By harnessing those tools, humans can navigate their busy lives with extra typical performance, productivity, and a experience of manipulate over their time.

The Pillars of a Time Management Plan:

A properly-based time manipulate plan is based on numerous crucial pillars. At the center is prioritization, where the reader is reminded of the importance of discerning amongst what is without a doubt remarkable and what is merely urgent. This act of prioritization serves due to the fact the linchpin for powerful making plans. Once priorities are hooked up, the plan can begin to take shape.

Aligning with Your Goals:

Aligning together along with your dreams is the artwork of connecting your every day actions, alternatives, and priorities together together with your massive objectives and aspirations. It's approximately making sure that every step you are taking, whether or not or no longer large or small, is in concord with the course you've got set for yourself. By aligning your every day efforts collectively together with your desires, you create a experience of reason and path on your lifestyles. It's a effective manner to make the most of it slow control strategies, as every mission turns into a terrific step within the route of the conclusion of your desires and dreams. This alignment guarantees which you're always shifting in the proper route, most important to a extra exciting and purpose-driven life.

The Art of Time Blocking:

The artwork of time blocking off is a time management approach that consists of dedicating specific blocks of time to specific duties or activities. It's about structuring one's day to make sure focused, uninterrupted artwork on the most important priorities. Time blocking gives a systematic method to dealing with time, permitting humans to allocate time to every professional and personal commitments. By embracing the art work of time blocking off, humans can enhance their productiveness, preserve better control over their schedules, and in the end obtain a sense of balance and accomplishment in their each day lives.

Mastering Scheduling:

Mastering scheduling is a key detail of powerful time management. Scheduling consists of the strategic allocation of time to precise obligations, sports activities, and appointments. When finished successfully, it guarantees that one's day is prepared, priorities are addressed, and dreams are met. Successful scheduling calls for putting clean desires, prioritizing duties, and growing a based totally plan that optimizes available time. It allows humans to make the maximum of their day, keep away from remaining-minute rushes, and keep a experience of manipulate over their time table. By studying scheduling, individuals can advantage more efficiency and productiveness, in the long run crucial to more balanced and high-quality lives.

The Power of To-Do Lists:

The energy of to-do lists lies in their simplicity and effectiveness in organizing responsibilities and priorities. To-do lists help people seize and shape the sports activities they want to finish, taking into consideration a easy, visible instance in their day's schedule. This practical device lets in people to control their time, lessen strain, and maintain attention via breaking down massive responsibilities into capability steps. By ticking off items as they're completed, to-do lists offer a revel in of fulfillment and motivation. Whether on paper or in a virtual layout, to-do lists are a critical aid in time manage, supporting individuals in staying organized and ensuring that now not anything crucial slips via the cracks.

Constructing a Weekly Time Management Plan:

This bankruptcy offers readers a sensible roadmap for developing a weekly time control plan. It walks them thru the way of evaluating their contemporary time allocation, putting particular weekly goals, and translating the ones desires into actionable responsibilities. By the give up of this phase, readers should be prepared with a custom designed, whole plan for the week beforehand.

Chapter 3: Eliminating Time Wasters

In Chapter four of "Time Management for Dummies," the focal point is on one of the most urgent disturbing conditions in effective time manipulate: removing time wasters. Wasted time is the arch-nemesis of productivity, and this chapter equips readers with the statistics and techniques to discover and dispose of the ones insidious conduct and distractions that thieve treasured hours from our days.

Identifying Time Wasters:

Identifying time wasters is a essential step in powerful time control. These are sports activities or behavior that consume time without contributing to at least one's goals or nicely-being. By spotting and addressing time wasters, people can free up treasured hours for more productive or massive endeavors. Time wasters can encompass excessive social media use, aimless net browsing, disorganized workspaces, or unproductive meetings. The capability to choose out the ones culprits empowers human beings to reclaim their time, streamline their sports activities activities, and enhance their normal performance and productivity.

The Pareto Principle in Action:

The Pareto Principle, frequently called the eighty/20 rule, is a effective idea that famous sensible software in severa elements of lifestyles, together with time manipulate. In movement, it technique that type of 80% of effects or outcomes come from absolutely 20% of efforts or sports activities activities. By figuring out the most large duties or sports activities within the 20%, humans can consciousness their time and energy on what in reality topics, yielding a disproportionate impact on their goals. This precept empowers humans to make knowledgeable choices approximately how they allocate their time, prioritize responsibilities, and optimize productivity, ultimately primary to greater green and effective time control.

Procrastination: The Silent Thief of Time:

Procrastination is a amazing time waster, and this chapter addresses it head-on. The writer delves into the intellectual elements of procrastination, explaining why people procrastinate and a way to fight this dependancy correctly. Strategies for overcoming procrastination encompass breaking obligations into smaller, potential steps, setting particular closing dates, and the use of time-blockading techniques.

Digital Detox: Managing Screen Time:

A virtual detox, or managing show time, is a exercising of intentionally decreasing one's use of virtual devices, which incorporates smartphones, laptop structures, and tablets. It's a response to the pervasive nature of generation in our lives. A digital detox can comprise putting obstacles for display time, designating tech-unfastened durations, and being conscious of how a first-rate deal time we spend on virtual shows. It allows in reducing digital distractions, improving productivity, and fostering a extra wholesome paintings-existence balance. By dealing with display time efficaciously, human beings can regain manipulate over their digital lives, lessen strain, and free up valuable time for special meaningful sports.

Email Management:

Email manage is a critical detail of effective time management within the digital age. It includes the systematic enterprise organization, prioritization, and green coping with of e mail verbal exchange. By implementing techniques like setting particular e mail-checking periods, the use of filters and folders to categorize messages, and the usage of the 2-minute rule for short responses, people can optimize their email manage. This not exceptional permits in reducing e mail-related distractions but moreover frees up valuable time for additonal massive and inexperienced responsibilities, ultimately contributing to stepped forward time manipulate and normal performance.

Mindful Internet Use:

Mindful net use is a exercising that includes being conscious and intentional approximately how we utilize online sources and era. In an generation of everyday connectivity, it is clean to emerge as distracted, overwhelmed, or possibly hooked on digital structures. Practicing conscious net use encourages people to set barriers, limit distractions, and be observed in their on line interactions. It fosters a greater healthful dating with era, decreasing the horrible impact of excessive display screen time on productiveness and common nicely-being. By being aware of the manner we have interaction with the virtual global, we are able to regain manage of our time and use the internet as a device for gaining knowledge of, verbal exchange, and productiveness, in preference to a supply of distraction.

Effective Meetings and Communication:

Effective conferences and communication are important to green time manipulate. Clear, concise conversation ensures that conferences are practical, productive, and time-green. By setting smooth agendas, speakme expectancies, and facilitating open and advantageous discussions, individuals can maximize the cost of meetings. Effective verbal exchange moreover extends to each day interactions, in which clean and well timed messages assist save you misunderstandings and decrease wasted time. Cultivating a way of life of effective conferences and communication promotes productivity and contributes to better time manage, in the end assisting people and corporations attain their dreams more successfully.

Time Wasters within the Physical Workspace:

Time wasters inside the bodily workspace are distractions, disorganization, or inefficiencies that consume valuable time and restriction productiveness. These can encompass cluttered artwork regions, frequent interruptions, and unstructured workflows. Identifying and addressing those time wasters is important for powerful time manage. By optimizing the physical workspace, human beings can reduce disruptions, enhance attention, and enhance their capacity to perform duties efficaciously, in the long run reclaiming treasured time for more full-size and green artwork.

Learning to Say No:

Learning to say no is a important capacity in time control and personal improvement. It entails setting limitations and putting forward oneself on the equal time as faced with requests, commitments, or duties that don't align with one's priorities or goals. Saying no allows people to protect their time and electricity for the obligations and sports that really rely. It empowers humans to avoid overcommitting, lessen stress, and maintain a experience of stability in their lives. By getting to know the art work of saying no gracefully and assertively, human beings can beautify their time manage, interest on their desires, and create vicinity for what genuinely aligns with their values and aspirations.

The Power of Routines and Habits:

The electricity of routines and behavior lies in their ability to streamline and automate our every day lives, making time manipulate greater inexperienced. Routines are dependent sequences of activities that provide predictability and consistency, decreasing choice fatigue. Habits, as an alternative, are computerized behaviors that, as quickly as mounted, require little aware attempt. Both workouts and behavior play a tremendous characteristic in time management thru assisting people create a disciplined framework for his or her day, making sure that important duties are finished with out the need for consistent decision-making. By harnessing the energy of workout routines and behavior, human beings can free up intellectual region, maintain hobby on excessive-priority sports activities

activities, and enhance normal productiveness and time control.

DELEGATION AND OUTSOURCING

In Chapter 5 of "Time Management for Dummies," the spotlight shifts to the artwork of delegation and outsourcing. As individuals juggle severa responsibilities and duties in their non-public and professional lives, it will become increasingly more tough to control time efficaciously without leveraging the electricity of delegation and outsourcing. This monetary catastrophe serves as a whole manual to getting to know the ones crucial talents.

The Power of Delegation:

The electricity of delegation lies in its capability to free up time and assets while leveraging the strengths and data of others. Delegating obligations and duties is a important time manipulate approach. By entrusting certain sports to succesful human beings, you may hobby on immoderate-priority responsibilities and desires. Delegation now not best will increase productiveness but also empowers group individuals and fosters collaboration. It is a valuable tool in time control, permitting human beings to reap greater, reduce their workload, and lead more balanced and powerful lives.

Understanding the Barriers to Delegation:

Understanding the boundaries to delegation is critical for effective time control and control. Delegation can be hindered thru various factors, such as a fear of dropping control, a lack of consider in others' talents, or the belief that positive obligations are too crucial to delegate. Recognizing the ones limitations is step one in overcoming them. By addressing the ones limitations through higher communication, abilities development, and constructing trust with institution humans, human beings can harness the energy of delegation to free up their time and cognizance on excessive-effect duties, in the long run enhancing their time manage and organization productivity.

Selecting the Right Tasks to Delegate:

Selecting the right obligations to delegate is a capability that would drastically beautify time control and productiveness. Delegation includes entrusting specific duties to others, permitting human beings to attention on more crucial duties. To make informed delegation options, it's far vital to pick out out duties which is probably a lot less crucial or can be finished extra correctly via someone else. Factors which includes the complexity of the mission, the skills and information of capability delegates, and the volume of take delivery of as genuine with and communique play a feature in selecting the right responsibilities to delegate. By studying this capacity, people can optimize their time manage, streamline their workload, and allocate their efforts to duties wherein they're capable of make the maximum brilliant effect.

Identifying Suitable Delegates:

Identifying suitable delegates is a critical problem of effective delegation, that could be a key time manipulate approach. It consists of assessing human beings inside one's institution or network who very own the critical abilties, records, and availability to deal with delegated duties. Recognizing their strengths and talents guarantees that responsibilities are delegated to the most certified humans. This approach not only lightens the workload for the delegator but moreover empowers delegates, permitting them to contribute meaningfully to the group's desires. The manner of figuring out suitable delegates allows for green project distribution, ultimately enhancing productivity and time manipulate for all concerned.

The Delegation Process:

The delegation device is a scientific method to entrusting duties and obligations to others. It entails figuring out responsibilities that can be assigned to human beings with the perfect abilties, providing smooth commands and expectancies, and tracking development. Effective delegation frees up time for additonal critical responsibilities and lets in others to boom their abilities. It additionally plays a outstanding characteristic in time manage, as it lets in people to recognition on immoderate-impact activities even as empowering a team to cope with regular or much less important obligations. Successful delegation involves smooth communique, don't forget, and follow-as much as make sure that the delegated tasks are finished satisfactorily.

Outsourcing: Leveraging External Resources:

Outsourcing includes delegating precise responsibilities or obligations to outdoor property, whether or not or now not human beings or agencies, to collect extra overall overall performance and effectiveness. It's a strategic method that allows individuals or groups to hobby on their center talents at the equal time as entrusting non-center features to experts. In terms of time control, outsourcing can be a valuable device to hold time and reduce the workload, permitting people to pay interest on duties that align with their primary dreams and information. By leveraging outdoor resources, feasible optimize time allocation and normal productiveness, making outsourcing an essential element of powerful time control and accomplishing favored outcomes.

Chapter 4: The Pomodoro Technique

Chapter 6 of "Time Management for Dummies" delves into well-known and effective time manipulate strategies: time-blocking off and the Pomodoro Technique. These strategies are designed to assist human beings shape their artwork, hold attention, and make the maximum in their time.

Understanding Time-Blocking:

Understanding time-blockading is fundamental to powerful time control. Time-blocking off is a technique in which human beings allocate particular, uninterrupted intervals for obligations or sports. By developing based totally blocks of time committed to incredible duties, humans can optimize productivity and interest. This approach helps individuals prioritize and achieve their desires on the equal time as warding off distractions. It's a realistic approach to coping with one's day and making sure that factor is spent deliberately on sizeable sports. Time-blocking off gives a seen framework for obligations, making it less difficult to adhere to a agenda and maximize performance.

Breaking Down Your Day:

Breaking down your day is a critical time manipulate method that includes dividing your every day agenda into possible blocks of time, each devoted to particular responsibilities or sports. By structuring your day on this way, you can allocate time successfully, making sure that essential priorities are addressed on the identical time as preserving a enjoy of corporation and attention. This method lets in human beings to technique their each day responsibilities with goal, making it much less complicated to manipulate their time successfully and save you responsibilities from turning into overwhelming. It empowers humans to hold a clean enjoy of path inside the direction of the day, ultimately main to advanced productiveness and a higher artwork-life stability.

Prioritizing Tasks inner Time Blocks:

Prioritizing duties interior time blocks is a key technique in effective time manipulate. It includes assigning a hierarchy to sports sports scheduled for a particular length, making sure that the maximum critical and impactful responsibilities are addressed first. This method permits human beings to focus on immoderate-priority gadgets at the same time as minimizing distractions and interruptions. By aligning undertaking significance with dedicated time blocks, individuals can maximize their productivity and make huge development closer to their dreams, growing a based totally and green framework for time control.

Maximizing Focus and Efficiency:

Maximizing consciousness and performance is at the coronary coronary heart of effective time control. It involves channeling one's hobby and efforts into obligations with precision and interest. Techniques including time-blockading and the Pomodoro technique may be treasured allies on this undertaking. By lowering distractions, putting clean dreams, and organizing one's art work, humans can enhance their productiveness and gather extra in lots less time. Maximizing focus and normal performance is prepared optimizing the use of available time and property, ensuring that every moment contributes to development and productivity in a unmarried's personal and expert life.

The Pomodoro Technique: A Productivity Powerhouse:

The Pomodoro Technique is a productivity powerhouse that has revolutionized time manipulate for hundreds. This method entails breaking art work into brief, targeted periods (normally 25 minutes) separated by manner of short breaks. These periods, called "Pomodoro's," are a strategic way to enhance interest and productiveness at the same time as preventing burnout. The method has obtained recognition for its simplicity and effectiveness, offering a based approach to managing duties, enhancing attention, and retaining paintings-lifestyles stability. By harnessing the electricity of the Pomodoro Technique, people can accomplish extra in tons plenty much less time and enjoy stepped forward time manage abilities with decreased pressure and mental fatigue.

Pomodoro Steps and Implementation:

The Pomodoro Technique is a time control technique that consists of breaking paintings into targeted durations (usually 25 mins) accompanied with the beneficial useful resource of short breaks. The steps for implementing the Pomodoro Technique are easy however effective. First, pick a assignment to paintings on. Set a timer for the one of a kind Pomodoro c language and artwork on the project with whole interest till the timer earrings. After completing a Pomodoro, take a short damage of five mins. Every 4 Pomodoro's, take an prolonged destroy of 15-30 minutes. This technique lets in enhance productiveness with the useful resource of way of leveraging the mind of targeted paintings and regular, rejuvenating breaks. It's a realistic device to shape work, keep interest, and manage time efficaciously.

Overcoming Procrastination and Distractions:

Overcoming procrastination and distractions is a critical difficulty of effective time manipulate. Procrastination frequently outcomes from severa psychological elements, at the same time as distractions can be outside or inner. To combat those stressful situations, people can enforce techniques which includes placing clear goals, breaking responsibilities into smaller, extra viable steps, and developing dependent schedules. Managing the digital distractions that generation brings and working in the direction of mindfulness can assist hold interest. By addressing procrastination and minimizing distractions, humans can extensively enhance their productiveness and make better use in their time, making sure that they achieve their dreams and priorities more effectively.

Customizing Pomodoro Intervals:

Customizing Pomodoro intervals consists of tailoring the well-known time manage method, the Pomodoro Technique, to man or woman options and goals. The widespread Pomodoro Technique recommends 25-minute artwork periods determined through using the use of 5-minute breaks, however customization permits human beings to modify these periods to higher healthy their attention and productivity styles. Some may also discover that shorter periods paintings higher, even as others may also moreover additionally benefit from longer artwork periods. Customization empowers human beings to check and find out the durations that maximize their productiveness and awareness. This flexibility is one of the strengths of the Pomodoro Technique, as it carries the uniqueness of absolutely everyone's paintings style and alternatives.

Combining Time-Blocking and Pomodoro:

Combining time-blocking off and the Pomodoro Technique is a dynamic approach to time manipulate. Time-blocking consists of scheduling precise periods for various responsibilities, at the equal time because the Pomodoro Technique segments paintings into centered periods followed via the use of short breaks. When used collectively, they offer a primarily based framework for productivity. Time-blockading allocates time for obligations and assigns priorities, whilst the Pomodoro Technique complements interest and usual overall performance within the ones time blocks. This mixture encourages disciplined paintings and ordinary breaks, essential to superior productiveness and a experience of success. It's a synergy that optimizes time control with the useful resource of manner of offering each shape and sustained attention in some unspecified time in the future of the workday.

Digital Tools and Apps for Time-Blocking and Pomodoro:

Digital gadget and apps play a significant characteristic in contemporary time manage, in particular in implementing time-blockading and the Pomodoro Technique. These tools provide the advantage of scheduling responsibilities and placing timers with precision. Apps like Google Calendar, Trello, and Taoist are first-rate for time-blocking, allowing human beings to allocate particular time slots for top notch sports activities. Additionally, Pomodoro-specific apps which consist of Focus Booster and Be Focused Timer help clients break their paintings into durations, improving interest and productiveness. With the combination of digital equipment, time manage will become more inexperienced and adaptable to the short-paced demands of contemporary international.

OVERCOMING TIME MANAGEMENT CHALLENGES

In Chapter 7 of "Time Management for Dummies," the focus is on the commonplace disturbing conditions that humans come across of their pursuit of powerful time control. This monetary wreck serves as a valuable aid for figuring out those boundaries and offers sensible strategies for overcoming them.

Identifying Your Time Management Challenges:

Identifying some time manage annoying situations is a critical first step in improving your productivity and universal performance. It involves self-awareness and recognizing the precise obstacles that ward off your capacity to manipulate some time successfully. These disturbing conditions can range from procrastination and distractions to poor employer and shortage of clean priorities. By pinpointing some time manage disturbing conditions, you can growth tailored strategies to address and conquer them. This self-popularity empowers you to make high-quality adjustments, streamline your workflow, and in the end benefit better time manage, allowing you to acquire your dreams and aspirations extra successfully.

Procrastination: The Ever-Persistent Foe:

Procrastination is the ever-chronic foe that plagues effective time management. It's the tendency to put off obligations however statistics their importance, often because of a choice for short-time period comfort or avoidance of pain. Recognizing procrastination is the first step in overcoming it. Employing techniques like setting easy time limits, breaking obligations into smaller, more potential steps, and locating motivation can help humans confront this adversary. Procrastination is an outstanding impediment, but with focus and attempt, it may be conquered, permitting human beings to reclaim their time and artwork inside the route in their dreams extra productively.

Time Management Tools and Technology:

Time control tools and era play a pivotal role in improving productivity and overall overall performance. These system, which range from virtual calendars and mission manage apps to undertaking manage software program program, allow people to higher put together their responsibilities, track their development, and set reminders for essential time limits. Leveraging technology for time management additionally gives the capability to get right of entry to and control one's time table from numerous gadgets, ensuring that essential commitments are in no way omitted. By embracing those device, humans can harness the strength of technology to optimize their time control practices, streamline their workflows, and make the maximum of their valuable time.

Interruptions and Multitasking:

Interruptions and multitasking can be huge time manage challenges. Interruptions disrupt workflow and attention, main to inefficiency. Multitasking, while apparently effective, can actually prevent overall performance as it divides attention and frequently outcomes in mistakes and delays. To manage interruptions, it's far essential to set clean barriers, restriction distractions, and communicate your availability successfully. Regarding multitasking, recognizing its boundaries and focusing on one challenge at a time can appreciably beautify productivity and the extremely good of hard work. By addressing those demanding conditions, people can reclaim their time, beautify interest, and beautify normal time manipulate universal overall performance.

Overwhelming Workload and Overcommitment:

An overwhelming workload and overcommitment are common traumatic conditions in time manipulate. These issues rise up on the identical time as humans cope with more duties and duties than they may efficiently manage. Overcommitment often stems from a choice to delight others or fear of lacking opportunities. However, it can bring about strain, burnout, and a lower in productivity. Managing an brilliant workload and overcommitment requires setting clean obstacles, analyzing to say no whilst important, and prioritizing duties primarily based totally on significance and urgency. By addressing those annoying conditions, humans can regain control over their time and obtain a extra wholesome artwork-existence stability.

Decision Fatigue and Cognitive Load:

Decision fatigue and cognitive load are crucial standards in know-how time control. Decision fatigue refers back to the depletion of mental energy resulting from making a multitude of choices sooner or later of the day, that could result in reduced effectiveness in selection-making because the day progresses. Cognitive load, as an opportunity, relates to the whole intellectual try required to device records and complete duties. Both of these factors can considerably effect one's capability to control time effectively. To mitigate choice fatigue and cognitive load, it is crucial to streamline sporting events, automate repetitive alternatives, and use time control techniques to make duties greater capability. This technique in the end consequences in more powerful use of highbrow assets and stepped forward time manage.

Managing Work-Life Balance:

Managing work-existence stability is the paintings of juggling professional commitments and personal life at the equal time as keeping one's nicely-being. It involves placing limitations, allocating time for every work and private interests, and ensuring that neither overpowers the opportunity. Effective art work-life stability contributes to reduced pressure, better mental and physical health, and stepped forward popular extremely good of existence. By the use of time manage strategies and embracing the significance of self-care, people can gather this stability, fostering concord and achievement in every their career and personal existence.

Stress and Burnout:

Stress and burnout are not unusual adversaries in the realm of time control and regular properly-being. Stress is the frame's herbal reaction to stress, at the same time as burnout is the stop result of persistent, unmanaged strain. In the context of time manipulate, unrelenting stress can keep away from productiveness, disrupt art work-existence balance, and lead to highbrow and bodily exhaustion. Recognizing the signs of strain and burnout is crucial, as is imposing strategies which includes rest techniques, time manage, and self-care to mitigate their effects. By addressing pressure and burnout, people can higher manage their time, maintain a healthy balance in their lives, and guard their everyday health and happiness.

Setting Realistic Goals and Expectations:

Setting sensible desires and expectancies is important in powerful time manage. Realistic desires are the ones that are possible within a given time-body and with available assets. It's critical to avoid setting overly formidable or not feasible desires, as this may reason frustration and burnout. By installing viable dreams and aligning expectations for that reason, individuals can art work methodically within the direction of their desires, hold a feel of fulfillment, and decrease stress. Realistic dreams and expectations are the constructing blocks of a sustainable and a success time control method, fostering a enjoy of control and motivation in a unmarried's adventure to accomplish their aspirations.

Seeking Support and Accountability:

Seeking help and duty is a valuable technique in effective time manage. It includes achieving out to trusted people, together with colleagues, mentors, or pals, who can offer guidance, encouragement, and remarks in a single's adventure to gain their dreams. Accountability companions, particularly, assist people live on the right track through regularly checking in on their development and keeping them chargeable for their commitments. This outside resource device gives motivation, glowing views, and an extended revel in of obligation, all of which make contributions to more successful time control and cause fulfillment.

Chapter 5: Technology and Time Management

Chapter eight of "Time Management for Dummies" delves into the dynamic and ever-evolving dating among era and time control. In the digital age, era performs a pivotal role in how humans prepare their lives, speak, and control their time. This financial ruin explores the impact of technology on time manage and gives sensible guidance for making the maximum of the digital tools at our disposal.

Embracing the Digital Revolution:

Embracing the virtual revolution is essential in modern day unexpectedly changing international. The introduction of era has converted how we artwork, talk, and manipulate our time. To correctly adapt to this virtual shift, humans want to no longer handiest include technological gadget and systems however furthermore cultivate virtual literacy. This entails harnessing the advantages of digital gadget for time manage, which include scheduling apps, assignment manage software program, and verbal exchange structures. By embracing the digital revolution, people can streamline their time control practices, decorate productivity, and stay agile within the face of ever-evolving era, ultimately predominant to more green and effective time control.

The Role of Digital Tools in Time Management:

Digital gear play a massive function in contemporary-day time control. With the arrival of generation, an array of applications, software program application application, and devices are available to assist humans streamline their duties, schedules, and priorities. These digital machine can aid in organizing, monitoring, and optimizing time, making it much less tough to manipulate complicated schedules and deadlines. From calendar apps for scheduling to to-do list software for challenge management, and assignment control gear for complicated endeavors, digital system enhance productivity and performance. However, their effectiveness moreover is primarily based upon on how nicely they are included into one's time management technique. Balancing their advantages with the potential for distractions is essential to harnessing the full functionality of virtual device in time control.

Digital Calendars and Scheduling:

Digital calendars and scheduling tools have revolutionized time manage. They offer a accessible and inexperienced way to plot, put together, and track obligations and appointments. Digital calendars offer capabilities like placing reminders, syncing during devices, and sharing schedules with others. These tools permit humans to control their time efficiently, making sure they stay on top of commitments, cut-off dates, and appointments. Digital calendars bring comfort and versatility, making it less hard to evolve to changing instances and preserve a nicely-based each day habitual, ultimately contributing to stepped forward time manipulate.

Task Management Apps:

Task control apps are digital equipment designed to help humans in organizing and optimizing their every day obligations and duties. These apps offer competencies like to-do lists, priority placing, reminders, and collaboration options, making them precious property for time manage. With the functionality to get proper of access to those apps on severa gadgets, clients can live associated and preserve their duties synchronized, improving their performance and productivity. Task management apps have come to be important in current-day time control, supporting users streamline their workflow, live prepared, and make sure that no vital challenge is ignored or forgotten.

Note-Taking and Information Management:

Note-taking and data control are critical competencies for powerful time manipulate and expertise retention. Note-taking includes taking photos vital facts during meetings, lectures, or studies, presenting a reference element for future movements and selections. With well-organized notes, people can rapid get admission to and assessment critical data, making it much less complicated to prioritize obligations and stay heading inside the right path. Efficient facts control, rather, ensures that notes are saved and labeled for clean retrieval. Utilizing digital gadget or physical filing systems can resource in coping with a wealth of facts. These skills in the end contribute to better selection-making and time optimization by means of imparting people with a dependable aid to refer once more to, supporting them make nicely-knowledgeable choices and execute responsibilities greater efficaciously.

Communication and Collaboration Platforms:

Communication and collaboration systems have end up crucial equipment in contemporary paintings environments. These systems embody pretty a number of software program and programs that facilitate communique, facts sharing, and collaboration amongst people and corporations, no matter their bodily area. From email and immediately messaging to venture control and video conferencing gear, the ones systems decorate productivity, streamline paintings strategies, and permit powerful teamwork. In modern-day-day interconnected international, they play a important characteristic in time control, as they permit for green coordination, real-time updates, and seamless sharing of records, ultimately contributing to progressed time manipulate and mission of completion.

The Art of Email Management:

he artwork of e mail control is a essential capability in powerful time manipulate, particularly in modern-day-day digital age. It consists of practices which incorporates putting easy conversation desires, organizing and categorizing emails, and imposing a based totally approach to coping with messages. Prioritizing emails based totally on importance and urgency, setting precise times for e mail checking, and the use of filters to govern incoming messages are all part of this artwork. By analyzing electronic mail control, people can reduce distractions, decorate productiveness, and make sure that their inbox turns into a useful device in area of a supply of constant interruption, taking into consideration more inexperienced use in their time.

Automation and Efficiency:

Automation and performance pass hand in hand, specifically in the realm of time manage. Automation involves streamlining responsibilities and tactics the usage of technology or systems, decreasing guide try and the danger of mistakes. It frees up precious time for more essential sports activities. Efficiency is about sporting out duties within the maximum innovative and effective way, getting rid of wastage of time and resources. Combining automation with overall performance empowers humans to cope with routine obligations with minimum attempt, leaving room for added impactful and modern art work. This dynamic duo is a powerful asset for everyone searching for to optimize their time management efforts, ensuring that point is used purposefully and productively.

Security and Privacy Concerns:

Security and privateness troubles in the context of time manipulate and generation are paramount. With the growing reliance on virtual tools and systems, human beings want to be vigilant about protective their personal and expert information. Safeguarding touchy information, together with schedules, venture lists, and personal records, is crucial to save you capability breaches. It's essential to apply regular and expert time manage apps, rent robust passwords, permit -trouble authentication, and frequently replace software program application to mitigate protection risks. Privacy problems moreover growth to the accountable managing of private statistics, making sure that it isn't always exploited for advertising or different functions with out consent. In an technology of developing virtual integration, handling protection and privacy in time control is an crucial part of retaining one's nicely-being and retaining control over private information.

Digital Detox and Mindful Tech Use:

Digital detox and aware tech use are important strategies in coping with the pervasive presence of generation in our lives. Digital detox includes taking intentional breaks from virtual gadgets to reconnect with the physical worldwide, lessen show show time, and alleviate the horrific effects of technology dependancy. Mindful tech use, then again, emphasizes the use of generation with consciousness, reason, and moderation. These practices are critical for maintaining a wholesome stability a number of the virtual and physical geographical regions, improving our interest, decreasing strain, and ensuring that technology serves as a tool for productiveness and nicely-being in place of a deliver of distraction and overwhelm.

Technology and Time Management Pitfalls:

Technology, on the same time as a valuable device in time manage, can also gift numerous pitfalls. Common pitfalls embody the temptation of normal connectivity, that could purpose distractions, overwork, and burnout. The regular influx of notifications and facts can disrupt attention and productiveness. Overreliance on era can also additionally result in a lack of face-to-face interplay and a lower in real-global stories. Moreover, the potential for digital dependancy and immoderate display display screen time can negatively impact physical and highbrow well-being. Recognizing and mitigating these era-associated pitfalls is crucial for keeping effective time control in the digital age.

Strategies for Managing Technology Overload:

Strategies for managing technology overload are crucial in our current, tech-driven global. Technology offers numerous blessings however also can bring about distraction and weigh down. To counter this, people can enforce techniques like setting precise deadlines for digital use, silencing non-critical notifications, and operating closer to virtual detox. Creating devoted era-loose zones or schedules can also help regain awareness. By organising smooth limitations and the usage of generation deliberately, people can mitigate the terrible results of generation overload, beautify their time manipulate, and hold a more wholesome stability a few of the digital and offline elements in their lives.

Integrating Technology into Time Management:

Integrating generation into time control is a contemporary-day-day-day vital. Technology offers a wealth of equipment and assets that can beautify productiveness, agency, and overall performance. From virtual calendars and undertaking manipulate apps to collaboration structures and communique tools, technology can streamline numerous factors of time control. By harnessing the power of generation, people can better plan their schedules, track development, and live related to colleagues and collaborators. However, it's vital to strike a balance and keep away from virtual distractions, using era as an resource in desire to a quandary to powerful time manipulate.

Cross-Device Synchronization:

Cross-tool synchronization is a technology that allows the seamless sharing and updating of records and data at some point of multiple gadgets. It ensures that human beings can get proper of access to their files, calendars, and wonderful digital property from numerous gadgets like smartphones, capsules, and pc systems. This synchronization simplifies time manipulate through way of deliberating a steady and up to date view of one's agenda and duties regardless of the device being used. It eliminates the need for guide records transfers and ensures that people have get right of entry to to the information they want, after they want it, selling efficiency and productiveness in an an increasing number of interconnected world.

Time-Tracking Tools:

Time-tracking tools are essential aids in powerful time control. These system may be inside the shape of software software program packages, cellular apps, or bodily devices designed to file and check how one's time is spent. They permit people to benefit insights into their each day workouts, select out time-losing activities, and make informed choices approximately improving their time management practices. By imparting a detailed breakdown of time allocation, those equipment empower customers to set goals, prioritize obligations, and degree improvement. Time-monitoring device beautify self-interest and are treasured assets for those searching out to optimize their productivity and make the maximum of every day.

Cloud-Based Collaboration:

Cloud-primarily based really collaboration is a modern-day-day approach to running together on obligations and responsibilities via virtual systems hosted on the cloud. It lets in humans and groups to get proper of entry to and collaborate on files, records, and conversation from anywhere with a web connection. This era fosters some distance flung teamwork, permitting actual-time sharing and improving of files, fostering conversation, and improving productivity. It's a treasured asset for human beings and agencies, facilitating seamless collaboration and inexperienced time manipulate through reducing geographical constraints and streamlining workflows. Cloud-primarily based completely collaboration has come to be more and more essential in modern-day fast-paced and interconnected worldwide, making it less difficult for humans to work together successfully and reap their dreams.

Balancing Technology Use:

Balancing generation use is important for effective time manipulate and retaining a healthy work-existence stability. In our more and more virtual worldwide, it is clean to grow to be crushed by means of using constant connectivity and display time. Balancing era use involves setting boundaries, being aware of show display time, and expertise whilst to unplug for non-public nicely-being. By handling our relationship with generation, we can prevent distractions, enhance reputation, and create vicinity for wonderful crucial elements of lifestyles, together with own family, amusement, and self-care. Achieving this balance permits us to harness the benefits of era on the identical time as safeguarding our time and mental health.

Accessibility and Inclusivity:

Accessibility and inclusivity are critical mind in making sure that everyone, irrespective of their skills or backgrounds, can truely participate and interact in severa components of life. In the context of time manipulate, it way making resources, equipment, and strategies to be had and person-nice for everyone. This guarantees that everyone can get entry to and benefit from time manage practices, regardless of their unique dreams and occasions. Embracing accessibility and inclusivity isn't only a remember of equity however additionally of maximizing the capability and contributions of a various range of people in accomplishing non-public and expert desires.

Cybersecurity and Data Protection:

Cybersecurity and records protection are paramount in contemporary day virtual age. With the growing reliance on generation, safeguarding sensitive information and private information is vital. Cybersecurity consists of imposing techniques and tools to protect toward cyber threats, which includes hacking, phishing, and malware. Data protection specializes in making sure the confidentiality, integrity, and availability of information, especially inside the context of privacy guidelines and excellent practices. These components aren't exquisite important for individuals however moreover for organizations to hold take delivery of as genuine with and safety in an more and more interconnected worldwide.

Digital Hygiene:

Digital hygiene refers to the workout of retaining a smooth and prepared virtual environment, usually targeted on digital gadgets, facts, and on line sports sports. It involves ordinary decluttering, powerful statistics control, and responsible use of generation. Just as non-public hygiene is essential for correctly-being, digital hygiene is important for excellent productivity and online protection. By managing emails, documents, and digital equipment correctly, humans can reduce virtual clutter, beautify their time manipulate, and defend their on-line presence from ability threats. Practicing virtual hygiene ensures that era stays a useful asset in desire to a supply of distraction or disease in a single's life.

Choosing the Right Tools:

Choosing the proper equipment in time control is a vital choice. It consists of deciding on the most appropriate technology, software software program, or strategies to help one's specific wishes and goals. The proper gear can decorate productiveness, enterprise, and performance. From digital apps for venture management to conventional techniques like time-blocking, the choice of gear need to align with an man or woman's selections and walking fashion. By making informed alternatives about the tools they use, people can streamline their time control processes, permitting them to make the most of their to be had time and resources.

Evolving with Technology:

Evolving with generation is an crucial element of cutting-edge time manage. In an technology where virtual system and enhancements constantly reshape the manner we art work and stay, adapting to technological changes is imperative. It includes staying updated on the modern-day era, mastering to leverage new gear for universal overall performance, and embracing digital solutions that enhance productiveness. By evolving with era, people can harness its blessings, streamline their time manipulate practices, and live aggressive in an an increasing number of digital global. It's about information that technology is a dynamic accomplice in our time management journey, one that we need to constantly test from and adapt to for you to thrive.

Managing Digital Distractions:

Managing virtual distractions is an crucial expertise in present day technology-pushed global. Digital distractions, together with social media, consistent notifications, and online surfing, can disrupt productiveness and time manipulate efforts. To fight these distractions, people can lease techniques like setting positive interest hours, turning off non-important notifications, and using website blockers. Practicing digital mindfulness, staying gift in some unspecified time in the future of digital interactions, and periodically detaching from technology via virtual detox also can help regain interest and control over one's time. By successfully handling digital distractions, humans can shield their productivity and channel their time and hobby in the direction of extra tremendous and precious responsibilities.

Digital Mindfulness and Focus:

Digital mindfulness and interest are important components of powerful time control inside the virtual age. They contain the deliberate workout of being virtually gift and attentive on the equal time as the use of virtual devices and technology. By working towards virtual mindfulness, individuals can lessen distractions, enhance attention, and save you time-losing sports activities regularly associated with technology use. Techniques at the side of placing particular desires for digital interactions, using equipment similar to the Pomodoro Technique to keep popularity, and operating toward digital detox to smooth the thoughts all make a contribution to superior virtual mindfulness and advanced time manage. This thoughts-set empowers human beings to harness the advantages of generation while maintaining control over their attention and time.

Project Management Software:

Project control software program application is a precious device that allows the planning, execution, and monitoring of projects and obligations. It permits people and groups to break down complicated projects into feasible steps, allocate property, set closing dates, and show display screen development efficiently. Project control software program enhances time manage by using providing a centralized platform for organizing, participating, and ensuring that everyone is at the equal internet web page. With skills like assignment assignments, Gantt charts, and development tracking, this software program software streamlines assignment management, making it an crucial asset for effective time control and productiveness.

Email Etiquette and Time Management:

Email etiquette performs a notable function in time control. The way we manage and talk via email can impact our productiveness and overall performance. Practicing ideal email etiquette, together with using easy and concise issue strains, organizing electronic mail folders, and respecting response times, can assist people preserve time and decrease the clutter in their inboxes. By successfully managing electronic mail communique, you likely can unfastened up valuable time and intellectual place to focus on greater important duties, ultimately enhancing time control practices and fashionable productivity.

Customizing Technology for Individual Needs:

Customizing generation for individual goals is a crucial hassle of powerful time manage. In the virtual age, technology plays a widespread characteristic in our daily lives, and tailoring it to our specific requirements can substantially beautify our productiveness. Whether it is customizing software program settings, growing customized workflows, or adapting apps to our alternatives, the capability to customise generation empowers people to art work greater efficaciously and align their digital equipment with their unique time control strategies. This personalization ensures that generation turns into a supportive device in place of a issue, helping us make the most of our time and obtain our desires with extra ease and precision.

Data Backup and Recovery:

Data backup and healing are vital components of time manage in the virtual age. These practices include frequently developing copies of critical digital information and establishing strategies to retrieve that information in the occasion of loss or harm. Effective records backup and restoration techniques provide peace of thoughts with the useful resource of safeguarding crucial documents, duties, and records from surprising facts loss due to hardware failure, accidents, or cyber threats. In a global wherein virtual records is crucial to paintings and private existence, getting to know information backup and recovery is important for maintaining seamless time management and minimizing disruptions.

Technology Training and Skill Development:

Technology education and know-how development are important components of effective time manage in the virtual age. As era continues to play a large position in our non-public and expert lives, obtaining the vital abilities to navigate digital system is important. Technology education includes turning into talented in software program application software program and apps that enhance productivity and time manipulate. It moreover consists of staying present day-day with growing generation. Skill improvement in this context empowers people to evolve to evolving virtual landscapes and make the most of available system. By making an funding in technology education and expertise development, humans can streamline their time manage practices, stay competitive within the modern world, and harness the entire ability of digital assets.

User Support and Troubleshooting:

User assist and troubleshooting are vital components of green time control in a technology-driven international. When human beings encounter technical issues or challenges with their virtual system or software program software software, searching out person help and using troubleshooting talents can prevent disruptions and wasted time. User help can include accomplishing out to customer support or consulting on-line belongings and forums for steering. Troubleshooting, however, empowers people to diagnose and resolve minor technical issues independently. Being talented in consumer beneficial resource and troubleshooting guarantees that generation remains an asset, now not a difficulty, in coping with one's time and responsibilities.

Cybersecurity Awareness:

Cybersecurity reputation is a critical trouble of effective time manipulate within the digital age. It involves knowledge and spotting the ability risks and threats related to on line sports and the safety of personal and professional information. Being aware about cybersecurity problems permits people to take proactive measures to defend their virtual belongings, thereby stopping disruptions of their schedules because of cyberattacks or statistics breaches. By staying knowledgeable approximately common cybersecurity threats, training safe online conduct, and frequently updating software software software and protection features, people can make sure that their time control efforts continue to be uninterrupted and that their digital lives are solid.

Staying Informed about Technology Trends:

Staying informed approximately era tendencies is important in our fast-paced virtual global. Technology evolves swiftly, and preserving up with the contemporary trends ensures that people can harness the whole capacity of virtual gear for green time control. By staying informed, humans can adapt to rising era and include them into their strategies. This records empowers them to make informed alternatives about which tech system are maximum suitable for their desires and to stay competitive of their non-public and expert lives. Staying informed about generation tendencies is an ongoing self-discipline that enhances one's capacity to leverage virtual improvements for powerful time manipulate and conventional fulfillment.

Chapter 6: Managing Personal and Work-Life Balance

Chapter nine of "Time Management for Dummies" delves into the sensitive and regularly hard task of managing personal and paintings-lifestyles balance. Achieving equilibrium between the desires of 1's career and private existence is a cornerstone of effective time manage, and this bankruptcy provides readers with a whole manual on a way to navigate this critical aspect in their lives.

Understanding the Importance of Work-Life Balance:

Understanding the importance of exertions-existence balance is fundamental for ordinary well-being and fine of lifestyles. Work-lifestyles balance involves engaging in equilibrium amongst one's expert responsibilities and private lifestyles, such as family, health, and amusement. It is vital for reducing pressure, preventing burnout, and nurturing relationships. A balanced life promotes physical and highbrow fitness, most important to prolonged productivity and undertaking pleasure. Recognizing the importance of hard work-existence balance is step one closer to making deliberate alternatives that prioritize personal time alongside professional commitments, ultimately enhancing the overall amazing of lifestyles.

The Evolving Nature of Work-Life Integration:

The evolving nature of hard work-life integration shows the changing landscape of approaches human beings stability their expert and personal lives. In extraordinarily-current global, generation, a long way off art work, and flexible schedules have blurred the boundaries among art work and private time. This evolution worrying conditions traditional necessities of exertions-life stability thru encouraging a extra blanketed approach. It method that human beings regularly discover themselves toggling among artwork and private duties, looking for techniques to harmonize each components in their lives. Adaptability, smooth obstacles, and powerful time manipulate turn out to be essential in navigating this evolving landscape to keep a experience of equilibrium and fulfillment. Work-existence integration acknowledges that life is a dynamic adventure, and locating the proper stability is an ongoing machine that adapts to the changing dreams of present day existence.

Setting Personal Boundaries:

Setting private limitations is an essential element of time control and maintaining a healthful art work-lifestyles balance. These limitations define the limits of 1's commitments and availability, ensuring that non-public time and nicely-being are safeguarded. By setting up clean boundaries among work and private existence, people can save you burnout, keep their intellectual and emotional health, and allocate their time in a manner that aligns with their values and priorities. Setting personal obstacles is an act of self-care, permitting humans to strike a harmonious stability among their professional and personal obligations at the same time as defensive their personal time and desires.

Time Blocking for Work-Life Harmony:

Time blocking off is a flexible time management method that is a endeavor-changer almost approximately accomplishing artwork-life harmony. By allocating specific blocks of time for artwork-related obligations, private sports activities sports, and self-care, human beings can create a structured and balanced time table. This technique guarantees that each expert obligations and personal well-being acquire the attention they deserve. Time blocking off offers a seen instance of 1's every day commitments, bearing in mind higher planning and stopping the intrusion of hard work into non-public life, or vice versa. By correctly the usage of time blocking, humans can craft a each day regular that promotes concord between their career and private life, in the long run enhancing their general nicely-being and pride.

Prioritizing Self-Care:

Prioritizing self-care is a critical component of effective time manage. It entails recognizing the significance of retaining one's physical and highbrow nicely-being for you to enhance productivity and simple extraordinary of lifestyles. Self-care encompasses sports activities which incorporates exercising, meditation, rest, and pursuing non-public pastimes. By allocating time for self-care, humans can recharge their power, reduce strain, and make certain that they'll be at their exquisite for tackling every day duties and stressful conditions. Prioritizing self-care isn't a luxurious but a want for sustaining a wholesome artwork-life stability and achieving extended-term fulfillment.

The Role of Flexibility and Adaptability:

The feature of pliability and versatility in time manage is paramount. In a worldwide wherein trade is regular, people who can adjust to evolving events are higher prepared to govern their time efficaciously. Being bendy permits for the lodging of sudden annoying conditions and possibilities, at the equal time as adaptability allows the change of strategies while desired. These trends no longer only save you frustration and burnout but additionally make certain that point manage practices stay relevant and a fulfillment in an ever-changing environment. Flexibility and flexibility function valuable tool, supporting humans navigate the complexities of cutting-edge life at the same time as preserving a enjoy of control and stability in their time control efforts.

Effective Communication:

Effective verbal exchange is a cornerstone of a achievement time control and collaboration. It includes the smooth and inexperienced trade of information, mind, and expectancies. In the context of time manage, effective communication ensures that dreams, responsibilities, and priorities are nicely-defined, and all and sundry involved is acquainted with their roles and obligations. This readability reduces misunderstandings, complements productivity, and minimizes the chance of wasted time. By fostering open and high-quality communication in each personal and expert settings, people can streamline their efforts, solve conflicts, and artwork together extra harmoniously, ultimately enhancing their not unusual time control and engaging in better outcomes.

Work-Life Balance Challenges:

Work-lifestyles balance annoying conditions are commonplace in modern fast-paced global. Balancing the desires of a career and private existence may be a daunting task. Challenges also can encompass prolonged running hours, heavy workloads, personal responsibilities, and the struggle to discover time for self-care and rest. Navigating the ones challenges frequently requires a mixture of time control strategies, setting barriers, and prioritizing one's properly-being. Recognizing and addressing paintings-existence stability traumatic conditions is crucial for retaining mental and bodily fitness and fostering harmonious relationships with circle of relatives and loved ones. It's a essential aspect of fundamental a satisfying and balanced existence.

Time for Family and Relationships:

Allocating time for family and nurturing private relationships is a crucial thing of work-lifestyles stability and powerful time control. Family and relationships are the cornerstones of emotional properly-being and average happiness. By setting aside devoted first-rate time for cherished ones, humans now not quality assist those bonds however moreover recharge and discover beneficial useful resource of their personal lives. Whether it's far spending time with own family individuals, keeping friendships, or nurturing romantic relationships, recognizing the importance of these connections and allocating time to nurture them is an crucial problem of a balanced and fun life.

The Art of Saying "No":

The artwork of announcing "no" is a critical potential in time manipulate and personal effectiveness. It consists of the functionality to decline extra commitments or requests when they do now not align with one's priorities, goals, or potential. By gracefully and assertively declining duties which can cause overload or detract from vital obligations, people can protect their time and electricity for what definitely topics. Saying "no" is not about being uncooperative however rather approximately setting barriers and making sure that one's time is used intentionally and in a manner that helps their dreams and well-being.

Reflection and Goal Setting:

Reflection and purpose putting are crucial components of powerful time manage and personal increase. Reflection includes searching back on one's achievements and demanding situations to benefit insights into what worked and what did not. Goal putting, as an alternative, is the way of putting in clean, particular goals for the future. These practices circulate hand in hand, as pondered photo informs the advent of giant, properly-crafted desires. Regularly reflecting on one's improvement and placing new dreams is a effective method to non-stop development and ensures that one's time and efforts are aligned with their evolving priorities and aspirations.

Mental Health:

Mental fitness is a essential problem of our simple well-being and an crucial detail of powerful time control. It encompasses our emotional, intellectual, and social nicely-being, and plays a large role in how we address stress, make picks, and relate to others. It's crucial to prioritize intellectual fitness because it right now affects our productivity, resilience, and our ability to govern time efficaciously. Taking steps to hold appropriate intellectual health, such as schooling self-care, seeking out assist at the equal time as preferred, and coping with strain, is vital to reaching a balanced and pleasant existence.

Delegation and Outsourcing for More Personal Time:

Delegation and outsourcing are strategic device for growing extra private time inside the realm of time control. Delegation consists of entrusting brilliant duties to others, whether or not or now not or now not at art work or domestic, to unfastened up some time table and consciousness on higher-precedence responsibilities. Outsourcing, but, includes contracting out unique responsibilities or tasks to outdoor specialists or offerings. Both techniques help human beings reclaim treasured time and reduce the load of handling every element themselves. By efficiently delegating or outsourcing obligations that can be dealt with by using manner of others, people can strike a balance among paintings and private existence, principal to improved non-public time for rest, amusement, and self-care.

Setting Clear Career and Personal Goals:

Setting clean profession and private dreams is a important thing of powerful time manage and existence pleasure. It involves defining specific, ability objectives in every expert and private domains. Clear desires provide course, reason, and motivation. They permit humans to prioritize obligations, allocate their time as it should be, and diploma their development. By installing well-described desires in profession and personal lifestyles, human beings can create a roadmap for success, make informed alternatives, and make certain that their each day actions align with their extended-term aspirations, in the long run essential to a extra high-quality and balanced life.

Embracing the "eighty/20" Principle:

Embracing the "80/20" precept, additionally known as the Pareto Principle, is a transformative method to time manipulate and productivity. It indicates that 80% of effects stem from 20% of efforts or motives. By recognizing this precept, human beings can find out the most impactful obligations or sports activities that yield the finest results. Embracing the "eighty/20" precept empowers people to consciousness their time and power on the maximum influential factors, ensuring that they make the most inexperienced and powerful use of their assets. This principle encourages a shift inside the path of prioritizing obligations that truly depend, in the end primary to more tremendous productivity and higher effects in various factors of existence.

Technology's Role in Flexible Work Arrangements:

Technology performs a pivotal characteristic in allowing flexible art work preparations, reworking the way we paintings and control our time. With the appearance of virtual equipment, some distance flung artwork, and telecommuting have end up increasingly more possible alternatives. Technology enables seamless communication, collaboration, and project control, allowing people to artwork from severa locations and adapt their schedules to better healthy their dreams. This flexibility gives numerous benefits, from progressed paintings-existence stability to multiplied productiveness. However, it also underscores the importance of the usage of era mindfully to hold a wholesome aggregate of labor and private lifestyles, emphasizing the position of digital tools in shaping cutting-edge work arrangements and the manner we manipulate our time.

Managing Work-Related Stress:

Managing paintings-related strain is crucial for effective time control and normal nicely-being. In present day speedy-paced artwork environments, strain can often keep away from productivity and personal existence delight. Strategies like setting limitations, prioritizing obligations, and operating closer to relaxation strategies are crucial in managing paintings-associated pressure. By recognizing strain triggers and using pressure management strategies, humans can keep their focus, decorate productiveness, and maintain their intellectual and emotional health. In doing so, they now not handiest decorate their time manage but moreover create a extra match and extra balanced paintings-life dynamic.

The Power of Boundaries in Personal Relationships:

The strength of limitations in non-public relationships cannot be overstated. Boundaries outline the limits of what is appropriate or cushty in any dating. They function a method to defend one's well-being, preserve individuality, and foster healthy connections with others. By placing and speakme clean barriers in non-public relationships, people can make sure their desires and values are actual, decreasing conflicts and misunderstandings. It's a critical aspect of maintaining art work-life stability, as non-public time and area want to be safeguarded genuinely as a good buy as expert commitments. Establishing and honoring obstacles empowers human beings to create a nurturing and sustainable framework for his or her non-public relationships.

Chapter 7: Continuous Improvement and Sustainability

Chapter 10 of "Time Management for Dummies" marks the quit end result of the book, focusing on the topics of non-forestall improvement and sustainability in time management. It underscores the concept that point manage isn't always a one-time venture however an ongoing journey in the direction of overall performance and productiveness. The financial disaster empowers readers to refine their time control capabilities commonly and preserve the nice modifications they have made.

The Journey of Continuous Improvement:

The journey of non-forestall improvement is a path of boom, getting to know, and evolution. It consists of the dedication to ongoing refinement and enhancement in numerous elements of lifestyles, which includes time management. Continuous development is a attitude that acknowledges that there may be typically room for growth and development. It encourages humans to include trade, take a look at from studies, and adapt their strategies as they evolve. This adventure is a lifelong business enterprise, marked with the useful resource of self-assessment, placing new goals, and a willpower to becoming the superb model of oneself. In time management, the journey of non-save you development fosters a life-style of overall performance and effectiveness, permitting human beings to refine their practices and preserve a satisfying and balanced existence.

Reflecting on Progress:

Reflecting on development is a vital practice in time manage and private development. It involves taking moments to evaluate one's adventure, spotting achievements, and figuring out regions for improvement. This self-evaluation is a precious tool for maintaining motivation and staying at the proper course. By pausing to mirror on development, people can adjust their strategies, refine their goals, and hold a smooth revel in of direction. This exercise not best guarantees that they'll be making effective use in their time however furthermore fosters a non-forestall willpower to growth and self-improvement.

Feedback and Self-Assessment:

Feedback and self-assessment are vital components of personal and professional growth. Feedback offers precious insights from others about our overall performance, supplying an out of doors attitude that lets in us recognize our strengths and areas for development. Self-evaluation, however, consists of introspection and self-evaluation, permitting us to benefit a deeper records of our personal abilities and development needs. Both feedback and self-assessment are powerful system for self-improvement and are key to refining time manipulate skills. By actively in search of comments and appealing in self-assessment, people can continuously adapt, examine, and enhance their time management practices, in the long run fundamental to more effective and inexperienced use in their time.

Setting New Goals:

Setting new desires is an important step in the adventure of personal and professional growth. New dreams offer route and cause, motivating human beings to try for non-forestall development. When putting dreams, it's miles important to reason them to specific, measurable, potential, applicable, and time-sure (SMART). These properly-described goals help humans live on path, diploma development, and align their efforts with their aspirations. Setting new desires maintains the course of self-improvement colorful and dynamic, making sure that humans are continuously jogging towards huge accomplishments and a more attractive life.

Fine-Tuning Time Management Techniques:

Fine-tuning time manage techniques is a essential a part of the non-forestall improvement way. It includes revisiting and optimizing the techniques and techniques one uses to control their time successfully. By paying attention to what works and what may want to now not, individuals can refine their time manage toolbox, making it greater tailored to their unique goals and occasions. This technique may additionally additionally moreover include adjusting schedules, experimenting with new techniques, and incorporating feedback from revel in. Fine-tuning time management strategies is critical for staying adaptable and evolving in one's time control adventure, ensuing in superior overall performance and productivity.

Experimenting with Innovative Approaches:

Experimenting with modern-day-day procedures is a dynamic and ahead-wondering method in time manipulate. It consists of looking for innovative techniques and clean views to address obligations and demanding conditions. Innovation can spark efficiency and productivity enhancements. By exploring new techniques and system, people can adapt to evolving artwork environments and live earlier inside the fast-paced global of time manage. This approach encourages a mind-set of interest and flexibility, in the end assisting human beings discover solutions that could revolutionize their time management practices and decorate their popular effectiveness.

Building Resilience and Adaptability:

Building resilience and versatility is critical in effective time manage. These tendencies empower people to navigate through surprising traumatic conditions, modifications, and setbacks while keeping their attention and backbone. Resilience permits for bouncing returned from disappointments and persevering within the face of boundaries. Adaptability manner being open to bendy techniques and embracing exchange as a natural a part of the adventure. In the sector of time control, resilience and versatility permit humans to live on course although topics do not go as deliberate, assisting them keep improvement and find out opportunity answers to reap their desires.

Sustainability and Work-Life Balance:

Sustainability in the context of difficult work-existence stability is ready keeping a healthful equilibrium over the long time. It consists of setting up practices and boundaries that ensure one's non-public and expert life can coexist harmoniously with out leading to burnout or forget about of each problem. Sustainability technique generally protective personal time, nurturing relationships, and keeping self-care physical activities. It's a reminder that paintings-life stability is not just a short-term fulfillment however an ongoing self-control to growing a fulfilling and balanced life that endures. Sustainability is the critical thing to reaping the blessings of tough work-life balance over the path of 1's profession and personal adventure.

Mindful Tech Use and Digital Detox:

Mindful tech use and periodic virtual detox are vital practices in ultra-modern digital age. Mindful tech use consists of being intentional and aware about how we have interplay with era, ensuring it enhances our lives in area of hinders them. It encourages setting barriers on display time, reducing distractions, and practicing digital mindfulness. Digital detox, as an alternative, includes unplugging from virtual gadgets for actual intervals to rejuvenate and refocus. These practices assist preserve a healthy dating with technology, lessen pressure, beautify productivity, and make contributions to powerful time control thru stopping virtual distractions from ingesting valuable time and attention.

Sustaining Healthy Habits:

Sustaining healthful habits is a important element of powerful time control and normal well-being. These behavior encompass practices like ordinary exercise, a balanced weight loss plan, exact enough sleep, and strain control. When blanketed into one's each day ordinary, healthy habits make a contribution to prolonged physical and intellectual resilience, which, in turn, enhances productivity and time control capabilities. Consistency in maintaining those conduct ensures that humans can maintain most high-quality energy ranges and intellectual clarity, facilitating their capability to cope with obligations and responsibilities extra efficaciously. By prioritizing and nurturing the ones behavior, humans can revel in a more in shape and more balanced manner of lifestyles on the equal time as maximizing their productivity and time manipulate capability.

Support and Accountability Partners:

Support and accountability companions play a vital role in time control and cause fulfillment. These are people or businesses that offer encouragement, steering, and shape to assist someone live on the proper tune with their desires. Support partners offer emotional and practical help, even as accountability companions maintain human beings liable for their commitments. Whether it's miles a mentor, a friend, a educate, or a coworker, having someone to percent improvement, setbacks, and milestones with can considerably growth motivation and effectiveness. Support and duty companions provide a sense of connection and reinforcement, making the journey of time manage and aim pursuit less daunting and further capability.

Celebrating Milestones:

Celebrating milestones is an vital workout in time manage and private development. It consists of recognizing and acknowledging the achievements and progress made along the journey closer to one's dreams. These celebrations may be each massive and small, serving as motivational markers of success. By celebrating milestones, individuals cultivate a nice mindset and keep their momentum, reinforcing the fee of their efforts. This exercise now not only boosts morale but additionally inspires ongoing dedication to the pursuit of large objectives, making the adventure extra profitable and exciting.

Chapter 8: The Psychology of Time

Time is a fundamental factor of our lives, governing our each day bodily games, selections, and research. In this financial ruin, we can delve into the psychology of time, exploring how our perception of time influences our conduct and nicely-being. By expertise your relationship with time, you may gain insights into your conduct, enhance time control, and ultimately lead a greater amazing existence.

Section 1: The Perceived Nature of Time

1.1 Subjective Time Perception:

Time perception varies amongst human beings. Some human beings experience time passing slowly, at the same time as others sense it dashing with the resource of. We'll discover the factors influencing those subjective reviews.

1.2 The Past, Present, and Future:

We'll check how people recognition at the beyond, gift, and future in a special way.

Understanding your temporal orientation can provide insights into your character and selection-making.

1.Three Time as a Psychological Construct:

Discuss how time is a highbrow assemble, and the way cultural and societal influences form our notion of time.

Section 2: Identifying Time-Wasting Behaviors

2.1 Procrastination:

Delve into the psychology of procrastination and provide sensible strategies for overcoming it.

2.2 Multitasking:

Explore the parable of multitasking, its impact on productiveness, and the way to shift to extra effective unmarried-tasking.

2.Three Perfectionism:

Examine the link among perfectionism and time-losing, and offer tips on a way to strike a balance between tremendous and efficiency.

2.Four Digital Distractions:

Discuss the location of smartphones, social media, and technology in time-losing, and offer techniques for dealing with virtual distractions.

2.Five Unproductive Habits:

Identify not unusual unproductive behavior that consume some time and power, which consist of immoderate conferences or lack of prioritization.

Section three: Strategies for Effective Time Management

3.1 Setting Goals and Priorities:

Teach the importance of putting clean goals and priorities to make the maximum of a while.

three.2 Time-Blocking and Scheduling:

Explain time-blocking off techniques and the blessings of creating based absolutely schedules.

three.Three Delegation and Outsourcing:

Discuss the charge of delegating responsibilities and outsourcing even as important to unfastened up some time.

3.4 Time Management Tools and Apps:

Introduce various time manipulate gear and apps that can help in higher time manage.

3.Five Mindfulness and Time Awareness:

Explore how mindfulness practices can help beautify a while interest and selection-making.

Setting SMART Goals

Setting goals is a essential aspect of personal and expert development. In this bankruptcy, we are capable of discover the concept of SMART dreams, which stands for Specific, Measurable, Achievable, Relevant, and Time-sure. By the use of this framework, you may boom your possibilities of fulfillment and accumulate your chosen consequences. We can also moreover even talk powerful intention-setting techniques that will help you placed SMART goals into movement.

Section 1: Understanding SMART Goals

1.1 Specific Goals:

Learn the importance of placing smooth and specific dreams. Understand how specificity helps in defining the famous final results.

1.2 Measurable Goals:

Discuss the significance of measurable desires, which let you music development and determine on the equal time because the purpose has been performed.

1.Three Achievable Goals:

Explore the concept of possible dreams, which embody the function of self-evaluation, sources, and practical expectancies.

1.Four Relevant Goals:

Understand the significance of relevance in purpose putting and the manner it ensures that your goals align at the aspect of your values and prolonged-term dreams.

1.5 Time-Bound Goals:

Discuss the want of placing time-certain desires, which encompass the blessings of putting in area time limits and timeframes.

Section 2: Goal-Setting Strategies

2.1 Identifying Your Goals:

Learn the manner to find out your non-public and expert dreams, and the placement of introspection and self-popularity in this manner.

2.2 Prioritization:

Explore strategies for prioritizing your dreams and focusing on the maximum important ones.

2.Three Breaking Goals into Milestones:

Discuss the benefits of breaking large dreams into smaller, feasible milestones, making the general cause more potential.

2.Four Creating Action Plans:

Understand the significance of movement plans in reason fulfillment, together with putting particular steps and techniques to reap your desires.

2.Five Monitoring and Adjusting Goals:

Explore a way to song your development, discover boundaries, and regulate your desires even as essential to live on course.

2.6 Motivation and Persistence:

Discuss the function of motivation and staying strength in conducting your SMART goals, and strategies for retaining strength of will.

Setting SMART desires is a effective tool for carrying out your favored effects in life. By making your goals Specific, Measurable, Achievable, Relevant, and Time-sure, you create a roadmap for success. In this financial disaster, we have got moreover discussed powerful purpose-placing strategies that will help you enforce SMART dreams in various factors of your lifestyles. In the following financial ruin, we are capable of find out the importance of adaptability and flexibility whilst running towards your desires.

Prioritizing Your Tasks

Effective task prioritization is a key ability for private and expert productiveness. In this financial ruin, we are able to explore effective strategies for prioritizing responsibilities: Eisenhower's Urgent-Important Matrix and the four D's - Do, Delegate, Defer, Delete. These strategies will help you're making informed choices approximately a way to allocate a while and assets efficaciously.

Section 1: Eisenhower's Urgent-Important Matrix

1.1 Understanding the Matrix:

Explain the idea of the Urgent-Important Matrix, which categorizes tasks based totally on their urgency and importance.

1.2 Quadrant I - Urgent and Important:

Describe duties in Quadrant I, which require instantaneous interest and why they may be critical.

1.Three Quadrant II - Not Urgent but Important:

Explain the importance of obligations in Quadrant II, which can be crucial for prolonged-term dreams however do now not have an instantaneous reduce-off date.

1.4 Quadrant III - Urgent however Not Important:

Discuss duties in Quadrant III, which may additionally additionally seem pressing however are not at once related to your key dreams.

1.5 Quadrant IV - Not Urgent and Not Important:

Explain why duties in Quadrant IV should be minimized or eliminated from your to-do list.

Section 2: The 4 D's - Do, Delegate, Defer, Delete

2.1 The "Do" Strategy:

Discuss even as and the manner to address responsibilities in Quadrants I and II by taking immediate motion.

2.2 The "Delegate" Strategy:

Explain a manner to delegate duties to others once they fall inside their information or responsibilities.

2.Three The "Defer" Strategy:

Explore the concept of deferring duties in Quadrants I and II, developing a conscious choice to cope with them later.

2.Four The "Delete" Strategy:

Discuss at the same time as and why it is useful to take away obligations from your to-do list, in particular those in Quadrants III and IV.

Section 3: Implementing Task Prioritization

3.1 Daily Task Management:

Provide steerage on a way to observe each the Urgent-Important Matrix and the four D's on your each day project manage.

3.2 Time Management and Efficiency:

Explain how the ones prioritization techniques can cause advanced time control and extended basic overall performance.

Chapter 9: Time Tracking and Analysis

Effective time manage requires an understanding of ways you presently spend some time. In this chapter, we're capable of discover the exercise of retaining a time log and the way to research a while utilization. By monitoring and reading some time, you could find out regions for development, make informed alternatives, and optimize your each day physical activities.

Section 1: Keeping a Time Log

1.1 What is a Time Log?

Define a time log as a document of the way you allocate it sluggish at a few degree inside the day, generally damaged down into periods.

1.2 The Importance of Time Logging:

Explain why retaining a time log is valuable for gaining belief into your each day behavior and figuring out inefficiencies.

1.Three Types of Time Logs:

Discuss specific strategies for maintaining time logs, collectively with digital gadget, paper-primarily based sincerely logs, and apps.

1.4 How to Keep a Time Log:

Provide step-by-step commands on the manner to start and maintain a time log, including placing durations and recording sports activities activities.

1.Five Consistency and Honesty:

Emphasize the significance of consistency and honesty at the same time as retaining a time log to ensure accurate facts.

Section 2: Analyzing Your Time Usage

2.1 Categorizing Activities:

Explain the manner to categorize recorded sports sports into meaningful organizations, collectively with art work-associated, leisure, non-public, and terrific education.

2.2 Identifying Time Wasters:

Discuss the manner of identifying sports that aren't contributing to your goals and are, in reality, time-dropping.

2.Three Evaluating Time Allocation:

Provide steering on assessing how masses time you allocate to distinct regions of your life, which includes artwork, family, and personal increase.

2.Four Goal Alignment:

Explore the manner to decide in case your time usage aligns collectively in conjunction with your brief-term and lengthy-term goals.

2.5 Making Informed Changes:

Explain the approach of the use of time evaluation to make knowledgeable picks about adjusting your every day exercises and obligations.

Section 3: Benefits of Time Tracking and Analysis

3.1 Improved Time Management:

Discuss how time monitoring and assessment can result in higher time control and expanded productiveness.

3.2 Stress Reduction:

Highlight how identifying time wasters and making modifications can reduce strain and enhance artwork-existence balance.

three.Three Personal Growth:

Explain how reading a while will let you attention on non-public increase and self-improvement.

Keeping a time log and studying it sluggish usage is a powerful practice for improving it sluggish management talents and making greater knowledgeable choices approximately a manner to spend a while. By understanding the manner you presently allocate it sluggish, you can make incredible adjustments that align collectively collectively together with your desires and priorities. In the following monetary disaster, we can find out strategies for overcoming not unusual time-related stressful situations and engaging in greater artwork-existence stability.

The Pomodoro Technique

In a global full of distractions and constant wishes on our time, preserving reputation and productiveness can be a venture. In this financial disaster, we can discover the Pomodoro Technique, a time control technique designed to enhance popularity, productiveness, and time control. By records and enforcing the Pomodoro Technique, you may make massive enhancements in your artwork conduct.

Section 1: Explaining the Pomodoro Method

1.1 What is the Pomodoro Technique?

Define the Pomodoro Technique as a time manipulate approach advanced through Francesco Cirillo, characterised through paintings durations (Pomodoros) and quick breaks.

1.2 The Pomodoro Timer:

Explain the use of a timer (generally set for 25 mins) to mark the start of a Pomodoro and sign a harm.

1.Three The Concept of Sprints:

Discuss how Pomodoros are used as focused art work sprints, providing set up, uninterrupted periods of labor.

1.Four Short Breaks:

Describe the cause of short breaks (generally 5 minutes) between Pomodoros and their characteristic in maintaining productivity.

1.Five Long Breaks:

Explain the concept of longer breaks (15-half of-hour) after completing a set of Pomodoros (usually 4), thinking about rejuvenation.

Section 2: Implementing Pomodoro for Improved Focus

2.1 Setting Clear Goals:

Discuss the importance of placing easy and feasible desires earlier than starting a Pomodoro.

2.2 Eliminating Distractions:

Provide techniques for developing a distraction-unfastened paintings surroundings within the course of Pomodoros.

2.Three Tracking Progress:

Explain how monitoring your Pomodoros and obligations assist you to examine your productiveness and make improvements.

2.Four Adjusting Work Intervals:

Discuss the way to tailor the period of Pomodoros to your personal attention span and electricity stages.

2.Five Combating Procrastination:

Highlight how the Pomodoro Technique can be effective in stopping procrastination and enhancing motivation.

Section 3: Benefits of the Pomodoro Technique

3.1 Improved Concentration:

Explain how the based totally artwork intervals of the Pomodoro Technique can enhance attention and reduce burnout.

3.2 Enhanced Productivity:

Discuss how Pomodoros can bring about elevated productiveness and assignment final touch.

three.Three Time Management:

Explore how the Pomodoro Technique can enhance time control via way of assisting you allocate time efficiently.

Chapter 10: Tools and Apps

In the virtual age, a big variety of time control gear and apps are to be had to help humans streamline their productivity and manage their time effectively. In this monetary catastrophe, we are able to assessment famous time manage tools and find out strategies for choosing the proper ones to suit your specific desires. By leveraging those machine, you can optimize some time manipulate and enhance your not unusual productiveness.

Section 1: Review of Popular Time Management Tools

1.1 Task Management Apps:

Discuss the functions and benefits of assignment manipulate apps like Todoist, Wunderlist, and Trello.

1.2 Calendar Apps:

Explore calendar apps which incorporates Google Calendar, Apple Calendar, and Microsoft Outlook, and the way they may permit you to time table and control some time.

1.Three Note-Taking Apps:

Review famous phrase-taking apps like Evernote and OneNote, and their role in organizing records and obligations.

1.Four Time Tracking Software:

Discuss the purpose of time monitoring software program application software like Toggl and Clockify, and the way they will let you reveal a while usage.

1.Five Project Management Tools:

Examine challenge manipulate gadget like Asana and Basecamp and their software program in handling complex obligations and obligations.

Section 2: Selecting the Right Tools for Your Needs

2.1 Identify Your Needs:

Discuss the importance of figuring out your precise time manipulate wishes and goals earlier than selecting a tool.

2.2 Consider Your Work Environment:

Explain how your artwork environment, whether or not or now not it is in an place of job or far flung, may additionally have an effect on the choice of time manage gear.

2.Three Compatibility and Integration:

Highlight the importance of choosing device which can be properly matched together together along with your present systems and may be seamlessly protected.

2.Four Mobile Accessibility:

Discuss the significance of mobile accessibility, permitting you to control your responsibilities and time on the glide.

2.5 User-Friendly Interfaces:

Emphasize the value of selecting tools with person-first-rate interfaces that fit your options and ease of use.

Section 3: Tips for Effective Implementation

three.1 Learning and Training:

Explain the significance of gaining knowledge of a way to apply your chosen time control device efficiently thru training or self-guided learning.

3.2 Regular Updates and Maintenance:

Discuss the need of preserving your tools and apps up to date and prepared for great universal performance.

3.Three Integration with Your Workflow:

Provide steerage on the way to mix your chosen tools seamlessly into your each day workflow for optimum performance.

three.Four Flexibility and Adaptability:

Explore the blessings of being bendy and adaptable in the use of it gradual control gear, thinking of adjustments for your paintings fashion and goals.

Time manipulate gadget and apps provide precious help in managing your obligations and optimizing your productivity. By selecting the right system that align collectively along with your goals and analyzing to apply them efficaciously, you could enhance a while manage skills and work extra correctly. In the subsequent economic wreck, we are able to discover strategies for keeping a piece-life balance and warding off burnout.

Planning and Scheduling

Planning and scheduling are vital factors of effective time manage. In this financial damage, we are capable of explore the significance of every day, weekly, and monthly planning, in addition to powerful scheduling techniques. By growing a well-established making plans and scheduling tool, you may maximize your productiveness, gather your goals, and preserve a healthful work-existence stability.

Section 1: Daily Planning

1.1 The Daily To-Do List:

Discuss the feature of a each day to-do listing in structuring your responsibilities and ensuring you stay on course.

1.2 Prioritizing Daily Tasks:

Provide steerage on a way to prioritize every day duties, emphasizing the significance of completing vital responsibilities first.

1.Three Time Blocking:

Explain how time blocking off can be used to allocate particular time slots for responsibilities and create a set up each day time table.

1.4 Morning Routines:

Explore the concept of installing location morning sports to set a pleasing tone for the day and beautify productiveness.

Section 2: Weekly Planning

2.1 Weekly Goal Setting:

Discuss the method of putting weekly dreams and the way they ought to align at the side of your longer-time period dreams.

2.2 Reviewing the Past Week:

Highlight the significance of reviewing the preceding week's accomplishments and areas for improvement.

2.Three Time Allocation:

Explain the manner to allocate some time at some point of unique obligations and responsibilities at some point of the week.

2.4 Weekly Planning Sessions:

Discuss the advantages of putting aside committed time for weekly planning durations.

Section 3: Monthly Planning

three.1 Monthly Goal Setting:

Explore the workout of placing monthly goals that align along side your prolonged-time period aspirations.

three.2 Monthly Calendars:

Discuss using month-to-month calendars to benefit a holistic view of your commitments and closing dates.

three.Three Reflect and Adjust:

Explain a manner to use monthly planning to mirror on your improvement and make vital modifications on your desires and priorities.

Section four: Effective Scheduling Techniques

4.1 Time Blocking:

Reiterate the importance of time blocking, emphasizing how it could be executed no longer only to every day planning but moreover to weekly and month-to-month schedules.

four.2 Batch Processing:

Discuss the idea of batch processing, in which similar responsibilities are grouped together to boom overall performance.

four.Three The Two-Minute Rule:

Explain the two-minute rule, which shows that if a mission may be finished in mins or an lousy lot an awful lot much less, it need to be completed immediately.

four.Four Schedule Buffer Time:

Highlight the price of which consist of buffer time to your time table to account for surprising events and keep flexibility.

Effective making plans and scheduling are essential abilties for managing it slow and conducting your desires. By imposing every day, weekly, and monthly making plans practices and using powerful scheduling techniques, you can create a based framework on your obligations and responsibilities, most important to stepped forward productiveness and a more wholesome paintings-lifestyles balance. In the following bankruptcy, we will discover techniques for strain control and retaining well-being for your time management journey.

Time Management inside the Workplace

Time manage is essential within the place of job to make sure productiveness and overall performance. In this chapter, we are capable of discover critical factors of time manipulate within the place of work: assembly control and managing place of work distractions. By mastering the ones skills, you can make the most of your artwork hours and make contributions to a more green and focused artwork surroundings.

Section 1: Meeting Management

1.1 Meeting Effectiveness:

Discuss the significance of effective meetings and the manner they impact productivity and time management inside the place of business.

1.2 Setting Clear Objectives:

Explain the significance of setting easy meeting desires and agendas to maintain discussions centered and green.

1.Three Time Allocation:

Provide guidance on allocating unique timeframes for conferences to avoid useless delays.

1.Four Attendance and Participation:

Discuss the significance of inviting high-quality critical people and provoking lively participation during conferences.

1.Five Follow-Up and Action Items:

Highlight the necessity of documenting motion devices and test-up plans to ensure that meetings result in actionable consequences.

Section 2: Dealing with Workplace Distractions

2.1 Identifying Common Distractions:

Discuss common place of work distractions, which includes email, social media, and noisy environments.

2.2 Time-Blocking for Focus:

Explain the usage of time-blocking techniques to allocate committed, distraction-unfastened periods for focused art work.

2.Three Digital Detox:

Explore the concept of a digital detox and its blessings in decreasing the impact of era-associated distractions.

2.Four The Role of Breaks:

Discuss how strategically planned breaks can assist refresh and refocus, mitigating the outcomes of administrative center distractions.

2.Five Establishing Boundaries:

Provide techniques for placing limitations within the place of business to lessen interruptions and distractions.

Section 3: Promoting a Productive Work Environment

3.1 Communication and Collaboration:

Explain the significance of powerful verbal exchange and collaboration in decreasing workplace distractions.

three.2 Clear Policies and Guidelines:

Discuss the placement of clear workplace guidelines and suggestions for managing distractions and retaining productiveness.

3.Three Time Management Training:

Highlight the rate of providing time manage schooling to employees to enhance their productiveness abilties.

Effective time manipulate in the place of job is crucial for both man or woman and organizational success. By getting to know assembly management and coping with administrative center distractions, you may create a greater targeted and powerful work surroundings. In the following bankruptcy, we're able to discover techniques for pressure control and preserving properly-being as you navigate the traumatic situations of time control in each your non-public and expert existence.

Time Management for Students

Time management is a critical potential for college kids, assisting them excel academically on the equal time as keeping a balanced lifestyles. In this chapter, we're able to find out time control techniques tailor-made for college university college students, focusing on powerful have a take a look at techniques and attaining a balance among teachers and extracurricular sports sports.

Section 1: Study Techniques

1.1 Setting Clear Goals:

Explain the significance of setting clear educational goals, together with examination education, challenge final dates, and lengthy-time period targets.

Chapter 11: Time Management for Parents

Balancing the desires of family and artwork life is a full-size assignment for parents. In this bankruptcy, we can discover time control strategies tailor-made for mother and father, focusing on correctly juggling family and artwork obligations at the same time as ensuring first-rate time with kids. By mastering the ones talents, parents can create a fulfilling and harmonious family life.

Section 1: Juggling Family and Work Responsibilities

1.1 Setting Clear Priorities:

Discuss the importance of setting up easy priorities amongst family and art work obligations.

1.2 Effective Scheduling:

Explain the use of effective scheduling techniques to allocate dedicated time for each circle of relatives and paintings commitments.

1.Three Communication and Collaboration:

Highlight the importance of open conversation along with your companion and powerful collaboration in managing own family and parenting obligations.

1.4 Delegating and Outsourcing:

Provide strategies for delegating responsibilities and outsourcing whilst crucial to maintain a balanced circle of relatives and work lifestyles.

1.Five Flexibility and Adaptability:

Explore the price of being flexible and adaptable in handling circle of relatives and art work duties, specially within the face of unexpected activities.

Section 2: Quality Time with Children

2.1 Creating Family Routines:

Discuss the advantages of making normal own family exercises that permit for high-quality time with youngsters.

2.2 Active Engagement:

Explore the idea of lively engagement with kids, which encompass playtime, shared sports activities, and massive conversations.

2.Three Technology-Free Zones:

Explain the significance of designating technology-loose zones and instances to promote extra massive interactions with children.

2.Four One-on-One Time:

Highlight the importance of spending one-on-one time with each little one to bolster the determine-little one relationship.

2.Five Being Present:

Discuss the rate of being sincerely gift and attentive even as interacting at the aspect of your kids, minimizing distractions from art work or other responsibilities.

Section 3: Promoting a Supportive Family Environment

3.1 Co-Parenting and Support:

Explore the function of co-parenting and looking for manual from prolonged circle of relatives contributors or caregivers in keeping a healthful family environment.

3.2 Time Management Strategies:

Share time manipulate techniques together collectively along with your partner to make certain every parents are aligned in handling own family and paintings responsibilities.

3.Three Self-Care:

Emphasize the importance of self-cope with dad and mom to keep bodily and intellectual properly-being, allowing them to better contend with their kids.

Time control for mother and father is crucial for creating a harmonious family existence at the same time as lovely paintings responsibilities. By effectively juggling family and paintings commitments, placing smooth priorities, and ensuring first-class time with children, dad and mom can foster sturdy family bonds and private properly-being. In the following financial disaster, we're capable of discover strategies for stress management and retaining famous nicely-being while effectively handling some time.

Time Management for Entrepreneurs

Entrepreneurship is a annoying adventure that frequently blurs the lines among organization and private lifestyles. In this monetary destroy, we are capable of find out time manage strategies tailored for marketers, specializing in balancing agency and personal existence on the same time as heading off burnout. By learning the ones competencies, entrepreneurs can acquire fulfillment while preserving their properly-being.

Section 1: Balancing Business and Personal Life

1.1 Defining Clear Boundaries:

Discuss the importance of putting clean boundaries among organization and personal life to hold a healthful stability.

1.2 Effective Scheduling:

Explain the use of effective scheduling strategies to allocate devoted time for each commercial enterprise enterprise and private commitments.

1.Three Delegating and Outsourcing:

Provide techniques for delegating duties and outsourcing even as vital to save you overextending your self.

1.Four Time for Family and Relationships:

Highlight the significance of allocating time for circle of relatives and nurturing private relationships outdoor of exertions.

1.5 Regular Breaks and Vacations:

Discuss the significance of everyday breaks and holidays to recharge and disconnect from artwork.

Section 2: Avoiding Burnout

2.1 Self-Care and Well-Being:

Explain the importance of self-care practices, along facet workout, relaxation, and stress control, to prevent burnout.

2.2 Time for Creativity and Innovation:

Discuss the rate of allocating time for creativity and innovation inside your business company to keep enthusiasm.

2.3 Time Management Tools:

Explore using time manipulate equipment and strategies to streamline artwork strategies and decrease the threat of burnout.

2.Four Regular Assessment:

Provide steering on often assessing your workload and commitments to pick out signs and symptoms of burnout and make crucial adjustments.

2.Five Seeking Support:

Highlight the significance of trying to find help from mentors, peers, and specialists whilst experiencing burnout or overwhelming stress.

Section three: Building a Supportive Business Environment

3.1 Team Collaboration:

Discuss the importance of fostering a collaborative and supportive group surroundings that could percent the workload and duties.

3.2 Effective Business Systems:

Emphasize the position of setting up inexperienced business enterprise structures and workflows that reduce the effort and time required for every day operations.

3.Three Business Strategy and Goals:

Explore how smooth agency techniques and goals can offer course and interest, reducing the risk of overcommitment.

Time manage for entrepreneurs is essential for sporting out commercial enterprise organization fulfillment on the equal time as maintaining non-public nicely-being. By balancing agency and private existence, setting obstacles, and maintaining off burnout via self-care and useful resource, marketers can thrive in their ventures. In the subsequent financial disaster, we are able to find out techniques for preserving a bit-life stability and primary properly-being for your time management adventure.

Chapter 12: Delegating and Outsourcing

Delegating and outsourcing are critical talents in effective time manipulate, permitting you to cognizance in your center responsibilities and obtain more productivity. In this bankruptcy, we are able to find out the art of identifying responsibilities appropriate for delegation and finding and dealing with outsourcing resources. By gaining knowledge of those skills, you could streamline your workload and maximize your overall performance.

Section 1: Identifying Tasks to Delegate

1.1 Task Assessment:

Discuss the significance of assessing your responsibilities and obligations to become aware of which ones may be delegated.

1.2 Core vs. Non-Core Tasks:

Explain the concept of center responsibilities (those without delay associated with your essential obligations) versus non-middle responsibilities (assisting obligations that can be delegated).

1.Three Skills and Competencies:

Discuss the manner to compare your personal capabilities and skills to decide the obligations you excel in and those better ideal for delegation.

1.Four Time Sensitivity:

Highlight the characteristic of time sensitivity in figuring out which responsibilities have to be delegated, specifically while dealing with tight deadlines.

1.Five Task Complexity:

Provide steerage on assessing the complexity of responsibilities and considering delegation for individuals who require specialized understanding or know-how.

Section 2: Finding and Managing Outsourcing Resources

2.1 Identifying Suitable Outsourcing Partners:

Explain a way to discover functionality outsourcing companions, along side freelancers, groups, and contractors.

2.2 Quality and Reputation:

Discuss the significance of comparing the exquisite and popularity of outsourcing property, emphasizing the want for reliable and organized partners.

2.Three Communication and Expectations:

Explore the significance of easy verbal exchange and placing expectations whilst strolling with outsourcing partners.

2.4 Contracts and Agreements:

Highlight the cost of formal contracts and agreements that outline the scope of hard work, deadlines, and charge phrases.

2.5 Project Management and Oversight:

Provide techniques for effective venture control and oversight when strolling with outsourcing partners to make sure a success collaboration.

Section three: Benefits of Delegating and Outsourcing

three.1 Increased Productivity:

Explain how delegating and outsourcing can reason improved productiveness with the aid of permitting you to attention on center obligations.

3.2 Time Savings:

Discuss how those practices can save you valuable time that can be allotted to extra important sports.

three.Three Specialized Expertise:

Highlight the advantages of getting access to specialised facts and abilties via outsourcing.

three.Four Scalability:

Explore how delegating and outsourcing could make your operations extra scalable and adaptable to adjustments in workload.

3.Five Work-Life Balance:

Emphasize how effective delegation and outsourcing can contribute to a more healthful artwork-life balance via lowering your workload.

Time Management for Creatives

Creativity frequently prospers on freedom and idea, however even the most innovative humans must manipulate their time correctly to stability revolutionary interests with day by day responsibilities. In this monetary disaster, we're capable of find out time manage strategies tailored for creatives, specializing in accomplishing this stability and overcoming current blocks. By gaining knowledge of the ones talents, creative humans can nurture their revolutionary endeavors at the same time as coping with their commitments.

Section 1: Balancing Creative Pursuits with Daily Responsibilities

1.1 Identifying Your Peak Creative Times:

Discuss the significance of recognizing your best and progressive times in the route of the day.

1.2 Setting Boundaries:

Explain how putting obstacles will will let you allocate time for progressive artwork at the same time as moreover managing every day obligations.

1.Three Prioritizing Creative Tasks:

Provide steerage on a way to prioritize progressive initiatives and obligations to ensure they receive devoted hobby.

1.Four Time Blocking for Creativity:

Explore using time blocking off techniques to allocate precise durations for innovative art work, preserving interest and area.

1.5 Flexible Scheduling:

Discuss the benefits of a bendy schedule that incorporates bursts of modern-day belief, even within a based ordinary.

Section 2: Creative Blocks and Overcoming Them

2.1 Recognizing Creative Blocks:

Explain commonplace motives of innovative blocks, which includes self-doubt, perfectionism, and burnout.

2.2 Freewriting and Brainstorming:

Highlight the fee of freewriting and brainstorming techniques to triumph over innovative blocks and stimulate sparkling thoughts.

2.Three Changing Perspectives:

Discuss how converting your mindset, surroundings, or medium can assist triumph over modern stagnation.

2.Four Seeking Inspiration:

Explore how searching for concept from numerous property, collectively with art work, nature, or different creatives, can rejuvenate your creativity.

2.Five Self-Care and Well-Being:

Emphasize the significance of self-care and maintaining properly-being to save you burnout and hold creativity.

Section three: Promoting a Supportive Creative Environment

three.1 Collaborative Opportunities:

Discuss how taking element with one in all a type creatives can provide a supportive and provoking environment for your paintings.

three.2 Feedback and Critique:

Explain the location of optimistic remarks and critique in enhancing your innovative artwork.

three.Three Time Management Tools:

Explore the usage of time manipulate equipment and strategies to streamline your modern-day device and preserve your reputation.

Time Management and Technology

In our increasingly more digital global, technology plays a substantial feature in each permitting productivity and offering distractions. In this chapter, we can find out the connection amongst time control and generation, that specialize in dealing with digital distractions and leveraging era for more appropriate productivity. By gaining knowledge of those capabilities, you may harness the electricity of generation to make the most of it gradual.

Section 1: Managing Digital Distractions

1.1 Identifying Digital Distractions:

Discuss common digital distractions, which includes social media, emails, and notifications, and the way they effect time manage.

1.2 The Role of Mindfulness:

Explain how running towards mindfulness will allow you switch out to be aware of digital distractions and their impact on your interest.

1.Three Digital Detox Strategies:

Provide techniques for enforcing a virtual detox, including setting unique boundaries and certain era-unfastened times.

1.Four App and Notification Management:

Explore the way to manipulate apps and notifications to your gadgets to lessen interruptions and regain manipulate of a while.

1.5 Effective Email Management:

Discuss techniques for green e mail manage, together with e-mail batching, categorization, and putting response instances.

Section 2: Leveraging Technology for Productivity

2.1 Time Management Apps:

Discuss using time control apps and tools to streamline your obligations and beautify productiveness.

2.2 Project Management Software:

Explore undertaking manipulate software program application and the way it is able to decorate collaboration and project organization.

2.Three Automation and Workflows:

Explain the blessings of automating repetitive obligations and developing inexperienced workflows to shop time.

2.Four Cloud-Based Collaboration:

Discuss the blessings of cloud-primarily based definitely collaboration equipment for far flung paintings and actual-time records sharing.

2.Five Personal Assistant Technology:

Highlight using private assistant generation, like voice-activated gadgets, to govern duties and access records rapid.

Section three: Striking a Balance

three.1 Setting Technology Boundaries:

Discuss the significance of setting easy obstacles with technology to keep away from overuse and digital burnout.

3.2 Utilizing Technology Mindfully:

Explain the concept of conscious technology utilization, which entails using generation with goal and interest.

3.Three Regular Assessment:

Provide steering on often assessing your technology conduct and making adjustments to preserve a healthy stability.

The courting among time manage and generation is multifaceted, with each demanding situations and possibilities. By effectively handling digital distractions and leveraging technology for productiveness, you may make generation a treasured pleasant friend on your time control adventure. In the following financial ruin, we are able to discover strategies for maintaining a chunk-existence balance and ordinary well-being

whilst efficiently dealing with some time in
our digital age.

Chapter 13: Stress Reduction

The courting among pressure and time control is apparent. Stress may be a sizeable barrier to powerful time manipulate, and horrible time manipulate can cause expanded strain. In this financial smash, we will discover the relationship among strain and time manage and provide techniques for lowering strain at the same time as optimizing a while management competencies. By studying those techniques, you may lead a greater balanced and effective life.

Section 1: The Connection between Stress and Time Management

1.1 The Stress-Time Management Loop:

Discuss how terrible time control can result in extended pressure, and, in flip, heightened strain can impair time manage.

1.2 Impact of Procrastination:

Explain how procrastination, a commonplace time manipulate hassle, can generate strain due to unmet time limits and very last-minute rushes.

1.Three Overcommitment and Burnout:

Highlight how overcommitment and immoderate workload, often a result of terrible time manipulate, can purpose burnout and chronic pressure.

1.Four Reduced Productivity:

Discuss how stress can decrease productivity and forestall green time manipulate.

1.Five Mindfulness and Self-Awareness:

Explore the significance of mindfulness and self-awareness in spotting the relationship amongst pressure and time control.

Section 2: Techniques for Stress Reduction

2.1 Time Management Techniques:

Provide time manipulate strategies, along side prioritization, delegation, and the Pomodoro Technique, to decorate productivity and reduce strain.

2.2 Mindfulness and Meditation:

Explain how training mindfulness and meditation can lessen strain via the use of promoting rest and awareness.

2.Three Stress-Reduction Activities:

Discuss pressure-discount sports activities like exercising, pastimes, and entertainment time, that could counteract the effects of strain.

2.Four Breathing Exercises:

Provide strategies for respiration sporting events to manipulate stress and hold composure in difficult situations.

2.Five Seeking Support:

Emphasize the significance of searching for assist from buddies, circle of relatives, or specialists while dealing with excessive ranges of stress.

Section three: Achieving Balance

3.1 Prioritizing Well-Being:

Discuss the want to prioritize private well-being, which encompass bodily and highbrow fitness, in undertaking a balanced and stress-free lifestyles.

three.2 Setting Realistic Goals:

Explain the significance of placing ability goals and boundaries to save you overcommitment and reduce strain.

3.Three Regular Evaluation:

Provide steerage on frequently evaluating some time control techniques and pressure levels to make crucial changes.

Time Management for Better Health

Maintaining accurate health is paramount for a satisfying and powerful lifestyles. In this bankruptcy, we are able to discover the connection between time manipulate and nicely-being, specializing in balancing paintings, workout, and nutrients. We can even delve into the important position of sleep and its impact on effective time control.

By getting to know those strategies, you may lead a more healthful and extra balanced lifestyles.

Section 1: Balancing Work, Exercise, and Nutrition

1.1 Prioritizing Exercise:

Discuss the significance of prioritizing ordinary exercising to sell bodily health and well-being.

1.2 Scheduling Workouts:

Provide steering on scheduling workout routines and integrating them into your every day or weekly routine.

1.Three Nutrition Planning:

Explain the importance of planning and maintaining a balanced food regimen for popular fitness and electricity.

1.4 Meal Prep and Healthy Eating:

Discuss the benefits of meal education and making more healthy eating alternatives, even during busy workdays.

1.Five Time-Blocking for Health:

Explore the use of time-blocking off strategies to allocate dedicated time for workout, meal planning, and self-care.

Section 2: Sleep and Its Impact on Time Management

2.1 The Importance of Sleep:

Highlight the important characteristic of sleep in preserving cognitive function, productivity, and primary fitness.

2.2 Sleep Hygiene:

Explain the idea of sleep hygiene and the practices that guide exceptional sleep, which consist of a normal sleep time desk and a conducive sleep environment.

2.Three The Connection Between Sleep and Productivity:

Discuss how insufficient sleep can save you productivity and the effective manipulate of time.

2.Four Power Naps:

Explore the advantages of electricity naps for a quick power beautify and extended alertness.

2.Five Balancing Sleep and Work:

Provide techniques for balancing paintings responsibilities with the need for good enough sleep to make sure most suitable time management.

Section 3: Achieving Holistic Health and Balance

three.1 Stress Management:

Discuss the importance of strain control strategies in promoting brand new health and time manipulate.

three.2 Regular Health Check-Ups:

Explain the cost of scheduling everyday health check-usato stumble upon and address capacity fitness issues.

3.Three Personal Well-Being:

Emphasize the need to prioritize personal nicely-being, at the side of highbrow health and emotional stability.

Balancing art work, workout, vitamins, and sleep is important for higher fitness and effective time control. By information the connection amongst time manage and nicely-being and implementing strategies to prioritize your fitness, you may lead a more balanced and efficient lifestyles. In the subsequent financial disaster, we are able to find out the concept of work-life balance and its importance in managing a while successfully.

Personal Finance

Effective personal finance and time control move hand in hand. In this financial ruin, we are able to find out the connection amongst time manipulate and economic nicely-being, that specialize in budgeting and economic planning, further to the strategic investment of time for economic boom. By analyzing the ones abilities, you could acquire greater financial stability and fulfillment.

Section 1: Budgeting and Financial Planning

1.1 Setting Financial Goals:

Discuss the importance of placing smooth monetary dreams and the way they relate to effective time control.

1.2 Creating a Budget:

Explain the technique of creating a charge range to song income, costs, and monetary financial savings, and how it enables control price variety efficaciously.

1.Three Regular Financial Review:

Highlight the need of regular economic evaluations to make certain which you stay on path collectively along with your monetary goals.

1.Four Time Allocation for Financial Planning:

Provide guidance on allocating devoted time for monetary planning, along with bill bills, charge range changes, and economic monetary savings contributions.

1.Five Automation of Financial Tasks:

Explore the blessings of automating financial obligations, which incorporates bill bills and financial savings contributions, to maintain time and keep monetary situation.

Section 2: Investment of Time for Financial Growth

2.1 Financial Education:

Discuss the significance of making an funding time in monetary training to make informed picks approximately investments, monetary financial savings, and debt control.

2.2 Building Additional Income Streams:

Explain strategies for building extra income streams, which incorporates facet agencies or investments, to enhance your financial growth.

2.3 Tax Planning:

Explore the function of time control in tax making plans to maximize financial savings through deductions and credit.

2.Four Long-Term Financial Planning:

Discuss the fee of allocating time for long-time period financial making plans, which includes retirement and estate planning.

2.Five Investment Strategies:

Provide insights into investment strategies and the importance of reading and monitoring investments to optimize returns.

Section three: Achieving Financial Freedom and Balance

3.1 Financial Discipline:

Discuss the characteristic of economic subject in dealing with prices, retaining off debt, and making the maximum of your assets.

3.2 Emergency Fund and Insurance:

Explain the importance of putting in an emergency fund and acquiring the perfect insurance coverage to shield your economic stability.

3.Three Regular Financial Assessment:

Provide steering on often assessing your monetary health and making vital adjustments to achieve financial balance.

Chapter 14: Long-Term Time Management Strategies

Effective time manage extends beyond each day duties and quick-term desires. In this monetary catastrophe, we are able to discover long-term time management techniques that target setting significant desires and growing a life plan. By learning the ones skills, you can navigate your lifestyles with motive and route, ensuring that it gradual is invested in sports activities sports that align at the aspect of your aspirations.

Section 1: Setting Long-Term Goals

1.1 The Significance of Long-Term Goals:

Discuss the significance of putting extended-term goals that offer a sense of purpose and path.

1.2 SMART Goal Setting:

Explain the SMART (Specific, Measurable, Achievable, Relevant, Time-positive) standards for putting powerful prolonged-time period goals.

1.3 Prioritizing Goals:

Provide steering on prioritizing extended-time period goals to make sure that they're aligned in conjunction with your values and objectives.

1.Four Goal Breakdown:

Discuss the manner of breaking down prolonged-term goals into smaller, achievable milestones to track development.

1.5 Goal Review and Adjustment:

Highlight the fee of often reviewing and adjusting lengthy-term desires to adapt to converting conditions.

Section 2: Creating a Life Plan

2.1 The Life Planning Process:

Explain the concept of lifestyles making plans and the stairs concerned in growing a whole lifestyles plan.

2.2 Values and Priorities:

Discuss the placement of personal values and priorities in shaping your lifestyles plan and desire-making.

2.Three Career and Personal Aspirations:

Explore how your profession and private aspirations are blanketed into your lifestyles plan, imparting readability in your course.

2.Four Balancing Life Areas:

Provide steerage on balancing numerous existence areas, which encompass family, career, fitness, and private increase, internal your lifestyles plan.

2.Five Review and Adaptation:

Emphasize the want to frequently assessment and adapt your existence plan as you progress thru one-of-a-type existence ranges and activities.

Section three: Achieving Long-Term Success and Fulfillment

three.1 Consistency and Persistence:

Discuss the significance of consistency and staying power in operating toward prolonged-term desires and pleasurable your existence plan.

3.2 Time Allocation for Long-Term Goals:

Explain a way to allocate time for your daily, weekly, and monthly schedules for sports activities that align at the facet of your extended-term goals.

three.Three Resilience and Adaptability:

Explore the features of resilience and adaptability in overcoming barriers and surprising disturbing situations to your route.

3.Four Celebrating Milestones:

Discuss the importance of celebrating milestones and achievements alongside your journey to preserve motivation and a experience of fulfillment.

Long-term time control strategies are the muse for a purpose-driven and fulfilled lifestyles. By placing terrific extended-term dreams, developing a life plan, and staying devoted to your aspirations, you could make the most of a while and paintings within the path of a destiny that aligns together with your values and targets. In the following financial catastrophe, we are able to recap the vital element requirements of powerful time manage and provide a roadmap in your persevered achievement.

Handling Time Management Challenges

Time control, whilst fairly beneficial, isn't always without its worrying conditions. In this financial disaster, we are capable of find out strategies for handling setbacks and barriers on your time manage journey. We may even delve into the idea of building resilience, it is essential for preserving your improvement in the face of adversity.

Section 1: Handling Setbacks and Obstacles

1.1 Recognizing Common Setbacks:

Discuss commonplace setbacks and barriers that human beings encounter in their time control efforts, collectively with unexpected activities, procrastination, or overcommitment.

1.2 Problem Solving and Adaptation:

Provide guidance on hassle-fixing strategies and adapting to surprising circumstances to reduce the effect of setbacks.

1.Three Time Management Assessment:

Discuss the significance of everyday time manage exams to discover regions wherein annoying conditions frequently get up.

1.Four Seeking Support:

Highlight the rate of searching out useful useful resource from mentors, friends, or experts while coping with chronic time manage stressful situations.

1.Five Mindset and Perspective:

Explore how a excessive quality attitude and a resilient attitude let you technique setbacks as possibilities for growth.

Section 2: Building Resilience

2.1 Understanding Resilience:

Define resilience and provide an cause of the manner it relates for your capability to get better from adversity to your time manage adventure.

2.2 Emotional Regulation:

Discuss the importance of emotional law in preserving a resilient outlook and handling pressure.

2.Three Self-Confidence and Self-Efficacy:

Explore how self-self assurance and self-efficacy make contributions to resilience and the belief that you could conquer challenges.

2.Four Support Networks:

Explain the function of assist networks, together with buddies, family, and mentors, in building resilience via providing encouragement and guidance.

2.Five Self-Care and Well-Being:

Emphasize the importance of self-care and well-being practices in nurturing resilience and maintaining a healthy mind-set.

Section three: Maintaining Progress

three.1 Learning from Challenges:

Discuss how setbacks and barriers may be valuable learning stories that make contributions in your growth in time management.

3.2 Flexibility and Adaptability:

Provide techniques for final flexible and adaptable for your time control method, permitting you to navigate disturbing situations extra correctly.

three.Three Setting Realistic Expectations:

Explain how placing practical expectations and dreams can prevent the undue strain which could reason setbacks.

three.Four Self-Reflection:

Highlight the importance of self-mirrored image in assessing a while manage adventure and making non-prevent enhancements.

Maintaining Work-Life Balance

Work-existence balance is a important issue of powerful time manipulate and frequently occurring well-being. In this economic disaster, we are capable of discover strategies for engaging in and preserving a balanced lifestyles, in addition to the importance of reevaluating priorities frequently. By mastering those skills, you can lead a fulfilling lifestyles that harmonizes your non-public and expert obligations.

Section 1: Strategies for Achieving a Balanced Life

1.1 Prioritization of Time:

Discuss the significance of placing clear priorities on your life to allocate time efficaciously to wonderful areas.

1.2 Time Management Techniques:

Provide steerage on utilizing time manipulate techniques, such as placing obstacles, delegation, and effective scheduling, to balance paintings and private existence.

1.Three Flexible Scheduling:

Explain the blessings of a flexible schedule that permits for adjustments as needed to stability paintings and personal commitments.

1.Four Quality Over Quantity:

Discuss the significance of valuing the remarkable of time spent in each paintings and personal life over sheer quantity.

1.Five Setting Boundaries:

Explore the idea of setting obstacles to shield private time and save you paintings from encroaching for your private existence.